TARTUFFE

MOLIÈRE

Translated, with an Introduction, by

ROBERT W. HARTLE

Professor of Romance Languages
Queens College of the City University of New York

• •

The Library of Liberal Arts
published by
The Bobbs-Merrill Company, Inc.
Indianapolis

Jean-Baptiste Poquelin, called Molière: 1622-1673

TARTUFFE was first performed in 1664

. . . .

The Bobbs-Merrill Company, Inc.
4300 West 62nd Street
Indianapolis, Indiana 46268

First Edition

Third Printing—1976

Library of Congress Catalog Card Number: 60-12946
ISBN 0-672-60275-X (pbk.)

CONTENTS
. . . .

TARTUFFE

Introduction

I

When Cardinal Mazarin died in March of 1661, Louis XIV was at last free to show publicly that he intended to be king in fact as well as in name. Whereas Richelieu and Mazarin had succeeded in breaking the power of the nobles, the religious parties had gained in temporal power. Even after the death of Mazarin, they continued to be strong, partly because of the influence of the queen mother, Anne of Austria, who had been regent for many years. Despite Louis' frequent protestations of respect for her, he coolly set about to destroy the power of her faction. In early September 1661, he ordered the arrest of Fouquet, the minister of finances appointed by Mazarin. Fouquet had merely been a bit more flamboyant in his malversations than most ministers, and he had the misfortune to wake up one morning to find that his downfall was to be a symbol of the king's absolute power. The poor man spent the remaining nineteen years of his life in prison. It is safe to say that the increasing openness with which Louis conducted his love affairs is also a good measure of his growing independence from the ecclesiastical faction at court. Until his mother died in 1666, he was obliged to disguise his attachments with at least some color of respectability, but, even so, most people at court were well aware that the long series of festivities called "The Pleasures of the Enchanted Island," held at Versailles in May 1664, was really given in honor of Louise de la Vallière.

At this two-week-long fête, Molière and his troupe contributed much of the entertainment. On the next to the last day, they performed for the first time three acts of a play called *Le Tartuffe*. Louis found the play "very amusing," but forbade its being produced in the future, because, the argument ran, credulous people might not make the proper distinctions and might feel that an attack was being made upon true piety rather than on the merely fraudulent. Actually, the king was privately somewhat puzzled by the sudden pressure put on him to suppress what he considered to be a harmless and witty comedy, but when the archbishop of Paris, and possibly the queen mother, personally remonstrated with him, he felt it prudent to give ground for the moment.

What Louis did not know was that almost a month before the first presentation of *Tartuffe* the secret Company of the Holy Sacrament had resolved to work for the suppression of the "wicked comedy." How they knew about it is still a mystery. This organization of pious laymen and clerics had begun with the laudable aims of suppressing vice and doing good works. Like most vigilantes, however, they tended to become institutional and to feel that because their aims were proper their vested interests constituted right. Since they were against sin, anyone not in agreement with them must be for it. Furthermore, like most such organizations, they must have had their hypocrites and opportunists. They were against *Tartuffe* on general principles, as they were against all plays, for they considered the theater to be a vicious institution; but this work particularly offended them because the villain derived his power through his position as a Director of Conscience, which happened to be one of their own favorite modes of operation.

In seventeenth-century France many rich and influential personages kept as a respected member of their household a Director of Conscience, who might be either an educated layman or a cleric. It was the duty of this person to soothe and purify his master's conscience by advising him how best to act in order to maintain a harmony between the abstract principles of religion and the specific cases that require action when one has executive power in this world. It is easy to see how a group of these directors, banded together in a secret society, could wield an influence disproportionate to their numbers and station in life. Their power had disquieted

Mazarin before his death and was obnoxious to Louis XIV. The Company of the Holy Sacrament was known contemptuously as "the cabal of the pious." The dark hints scattered throughout the play that Tartuffe has behind him a dangerous cabal, capable of trapping Orgon at every turn, must have seemed to the Company to be an open attack, as they no doubt were.

There were Jesuits among the Company of the Holy Sacrament, but the Jesuits as a whole had another reason to feel that they were being especially singled out for attack in *Tartuffe*—because of its references to casuistry. Casuistry, the art of adapting the spirit of a principle to specific *cases,* is necessary in order to live under any set of religious or ethical principles. No Christian, for example, would consider it an offense against the Eighth Commandment to steal a revolver from a would-be suicide, but unfortunately most of life's occasions are much less sharply defined. In any human affair, the means and the ends are always busily corrupting each other, making the measurement and establishment of moral tolerances infinitely delicate. These problems seem to have occurred with sudden urgency to the Spanish Jesuit clergy during the latter part of the sixteenth and the early part of the seventeenth century. Dozens of books poured forth, a late flowering of medieval scholasticism. Although it would be a false oversimplification to say that those works were written to keep people within the Church by proving that with a few legalisms one could do as one pleased without sinning, it is certain that to a large extent the wide diffusion of these books was based upon some such popular feeling. When, in 1656–1657, Pascal indignantly attacked casuistry and the Jesuits with his *Provincial Letters,* Escobar's 900-page treatise on *Moral Theology*—in which were classified and explained "the decisions of twenty-four casuists of the Society of Jesus"—had already gone rapidly through some forty editions. With the *Provincial Letters,* the public came to equate casuistry and its corollary, the direction of intention, with the Jesuits and an easygoing moral code. Thus, it seemed clear to everyone that

Molière was throwing a barb at the Jesuits when, in Act Four, Tartuffe says to Elmire:

> . . . I know the art of removing scruples.
> Heaven forbids—it's true—certain satisfactions;
> But one can arrange a give-and-take settlement.
> According to differing needs, there is a science
> Of stretching the fetters of our conscience,
> And rectifying the evil of the action
> With the purity of our intention.

With the performance of *Tartuffe*, Molière found himself involved in a bitter struggle with powerful and elusive enemies. The next few years were filled with petitions to the king, private readings and performances before the greatest of the nobility, at least two fundamental reworkings of the play, despair, and finally triumph. Why did Molière put so much time and effort into fighting this battle? Was it the creator's natural affection for his own creation? Was it because his troupe badly needed a successful play? Did he feel that he was fighting for the theater's freedom against the forces of bigotry? At various times, literary historians have championed one or another of these motives, excluding all the others. The truth, no doubt, is that Molière was a more complex individual than his literary historians suppose, and that all these motives—and perhaps some of which we are ignorant—played a part in his attitude. Certainly the commercial motive was present; the interdiction suddenly left his troupe with no novelty to produce except a bad first play by the then-unknown Jean Racine. Furthermore, Molière must have known that *Tartuffe*, when finally produced, would have the *succès de scandale* that it did achieve. On the other hand, it is certain that Molière became involved personally in the fight. Twice before, in his earlier career, he had been the victim of the machinations of the "Cabal of the Pious," and there is no mistaking the note of sincere discouragement in his second petition, in which he says to the king, "I can no longer think of writing comedies if the Tartuffes get the upper hand." (These words may, of course, also have been a discreet threat from the man who knew he was the king's favorite entertainer.) And Molière's personal bitterness against those he considered hypocrites shows very clearly through the fabric of the final scenes of *Dom Juan,* produced the following year.

Had it not been for the King's encouragement, Molière would certainly have found it necessary to give up the fight. In 1665, Louis XIV gave to Molière's troupe the title "king's troupe" and with it an annual pension of six thousand *livres.* Earlier, when a certain curé named Pierre Roullé—perhaps taking the interdiction of the play to mean more than it did —wrote a pamphlet in which Molière was described as "a demon dressed in flesh" and hardly fit for burning, the curé was made to feel royal displeasure at this work of supererogation. In 1667, the king apparently gave Molière verbal permission to present *The Impostor,* a considerably toned-down version of the play, in which Tartuffe—now become Panulphe— is a man of the world with laces and a sword, rather than a semicleric. Meanwhile, however, the king had left to command the army in Flanders, and the president of the Paris *parlement* was in charge of the police function. On the day following the opening of *The Impostor,* the president forbade its further presentation, and less than a week later Louis' former tutor, Hardouin de Péréfixe, now archbishop of Paris, issued an order forbidding all his diocesans "to present, read, or hear the above-named comedy . . . and this under penalty of excommunication." This was a heavy blow—one which even the king did not dare affront. It was not until early in 1669, with a new pope and the so-called "Peace of the Church," which gave Louis a much stronger hand than he had before, that Molière was finally able to present *Tartuffe* as we know it to-day. Its presentation was proof that, for the moment, the king dominated even the religious factions. The play was an instant and overwhelming success, and a durable one, too—of all the plays in the classic repertory it has been the most frequently performed.

II

What were the other two versions of *Tartuffe* like? We do not possess a text for either of them, although a *Letter on the Impostor,* inspired by Molière or one of his partisans, shows that the 1667 version was fairly close to the present text. The problem of the original *Tartuffe* has been the subject of violent critical disagreement for many years. Roughly, the opposing positions are these: One side contends that Molière presented the first three acts of the unfinished play in order to test the reaction before going any further; the other group claims that in 1664 the play was complete in three acts, and that the present version is an amplification and softening of the original. The principal basis for the former opinion has consisted of entries in the *Register* of La Grange, a member of Molière's troupe. The entry for May 12, 1664, recording what was played at court, adds, "and three acts of *Tartuffe,* which were the first three." The entry for September 25 of the same year speaks of "the first three acts of *Tartuffe.*" Opposing critics have maintained that it was against Molière's lifelong practice to present an unfinished play, that he preferred to finish a play in prose if necessary. Moreover, if the play had been unfinished at the time it was attacked so heavily, why didn't Molière or his partisans ever use the argument that would have been so telling, namely, that his opponents were being unfair in attacking an unfinished work? Furthermore, the first three acts cannot stand alone with any kind of artistic unity; it would be absurd to present a truncated play on a high court occasion. To all of which the strict literary historians have in effect replied, "All that makes sense, but documents are documents."

Recently, John Cairncross, in a book entitled *New Light on Molière,*[1] has carefully studied the documents and arrived at a common-sense interpretation that reconciles the apparent

[1] Geneva: Droz, 1956.

contradictions. He points out, for instance, what should have been evident immediately, that the entry in La Grange's *Register* could not have been contemporaneous with the three-act performance at Versailles because by its wording it presupposes the existence of the five-act play, which condition did not obtain until more than three years later. By many examples of entries that jump ahead in time Cairncross clearly shows that the *Register* was copied out, with amplifications, from jottings now lost. It is his opinion that it was written all at once in 1685 or 1687. If, then, these documents are reminiscences from scanty notes made more than twenty years before and concerning an extremely turbulent moment in the troupe's career, they lose most of their claim to unquestionable authenticity. There is no point in trying to reproduce all of Cairncross's arguments; they have, let us hope, established once and for all that the play was complete in three acts in 1664.

But which three acts were they? One opinion holds that the play was in the nature of a somewhat bitter burlesque, like *George Dandin,* in which the booby, in this case Orgon, is totally duped. Elmire would have a certain inclination toward Tartuffe, and the curtain line of the play would be Orgon's: "No, in spite of them all, you will keep her [Elmire] company. To drive people to fury is my greatest joy, and I want you to be seen with her constantly." Perhaps there would even be the donation, and the curtain would fall as Tartuffe says, "May heaven's will be done in all things." A strong argument in support of this theory maintains that, because there is no unmasking—no poetic justice—the play would easily give rise, in a French audience, to skeptical reflections about the true nature of all apparently devout practitioners. Thus, alarm among the religious party would be better motivated and more understandable than it would be from the play as it is known today.

John Cairncross proceeds quite differently. He points out, with a good deal of reason, that Act Two is mainly spent developing a subplot which is not straightened out until Act Five, and everyone agrees that Act Five was an afterthought added in order to rally the king's support. Hence, if the play consisted of the first three acts, the whole problem of Mariane and Valère would be left unresolved. Furthermore, while it is daring and effective to postpone Tartuffe's entrance until Act Three in a five-act play, it would be unthinkable in a three-act play. Cairncross reasons that the original version consisted of Acts One, Three, and Four in approximately the form in which they are known today. If Tartuffe is deprived of his hold over Orgon through possession of the strongbox— an event which occurs, rather lamely, in the closing lines of Act Four, and provides the motive for most of Act Five—then Orgon can order him out of the house and the play can end happily with the traitor unmasked and the dupe enlightened. The climax of the play is much more rollicking and light-hearted, as it coincides with the wonderful scene in which Orgon is hidden under the table. It is hard to believe that Molière did not think of this scene in his original conception of the play. Cairncross' hypothesis has the added advantage of presenting us with a much more coherent work of art, embodying themes and techniques—such as the unmasking—close to the core of the rest of Molière's production.

III

Whatever the exact form of the original *Tartuffe*, the same aesthetic problem arises: Can a play written and rewritten under such circumstances display any degree of organic unity? When discussing a writer of Molière's creative genius it is always prudent to assume a priori that the work is an artistic whole until the contrary be proved. There is no reason to assume that the total conception of the play did not shift to conform to the additions and changes Molière successively made.

Let us take, for example, Act Two, one of those that Cairncross believes to have been a later addition, because "Most critics regard the act as mere padding and stress the looseness of the connection between it and the main plot." [2] To refer

[2] *New Light on Molière*, p. 34.

to one-fifth of a play as "mere padding" is a serious aesthetic charge that merits further examination. The main contribution of Act Two to the plot is to supply the motive for Elmire's urgent intercession with Tartuffe in the following act; and it is certainly true that, if he wished, Molière could have presented Orgon's plan to marry off Mariane much more economically. However, most critics will agree that it is just as important to examine a part of a play for its *thematic* relations to the whole, and also for its function in establishing a rapport between the audience and the action, as it is to examine a part for its relationships to the outline of the plot.

Perhaps the essential seriousness of theme in Act Two has been frequently overlooked because it is fully dramatized in the comic mode. Molière's deftness never allows the tone to degenerate into maudlin sentimentality, even though the project of wedding Mariane to Tartuffe might easily have furnished the occasion for causing the audience to become passionately involved in the outcome. Instead, Molière evokes a bemused, almost condescending compassion for Mariane and Valère in their childish lovers' quarrel. This is the stuff of real humor. Even when Mariane announces her desperate plan of suicide, the audience smiles, because in Dorine's wit Molière provides the antidote to preserve the spectator's necessary detachment.

Although Molière presents these events in the comic mode, the viewer should not be blinded to the fact that, for the characters in the play, in the reality of their own world, all of these situations are very serious, and the playwright has only to make a slight shift in tone—as he does at the end of Act Four and the beginning of Act Five—to reveal the bleak devastation that has taken place in this small world through Tartuffe's corrosive influence. In this sense, the members of the audience are the real dupes of the play. In Orgon, Molière presents a clear picture of a sensible man led astray by his better instincts. We see corruption of the absolute power in this microcosm, naked tyranny going so far as to dispose of the *person* of another, and, finally, power degenerating to the ultimate point of fatuousness, as it gives to another its essential attributes. At this moment Molière, the master prestidigitator, draws back the comic veil, checks our laughter, and reminds us that the steps leading up to this atrocious situation have taken place in the very presence of our amusement. In Act One, Molière showed the master turned silly; in Act Two, he shows us the master turned surly. Dorine demonstrates that a wrathful tyrant is easier to handle than one with his wits about him; but, like any other bearbaiting, this situation, while funny for the moment, may end badly. All of these scenes in Act Two seem to be essential for an orderly development of the underlying themes of the play; furthermore, in this play that is so centrally concerned with power, corruption, and tyranny, Mariane shows us—although we may smile at the way in which she frames her resolve—that force has its limits, that only the individual himself can dispose of his person, although a tragic option may be required to prove it.

Students often object to the sudden and improbable denouement of *Tartuffe*. They seem to feel morally indignant that a *foreign* masterpiece should attempt a happy ending. To which a Frenchman might reply, "Which is more improbable, a sudden reversal brought about by the conversion of wicked characters—as happens not too infrequently on the Anglo-Saxon stage—or the improbable intervention of external force? Should Tartuffe—like Saint Genesius, the actor—find that his counterfeit piety has become the real thing and repent?" The only *realistic* course would end in domestic tragedy, for as the action proceeds the full weight of attention rests on each character in turn, and in each is discovered a secret flaw which prevents him from resolving the situation. For example, Cléante, who states so cogently the ethical core of the play, lacks executive strength; and Elmire, who finally maneuvers Tartuffe into a trap, acts too late. (Reason is pathetically powerless, and Truth must wear a mask.) Short of tragedy, then, the only possible solution to a situation in which local authority has been hoodwinked is the intervention of a more comprehensive power. And a change of tone from aristocratic comedy to bourgeois tragedy would be an unthinkable wrench. None of the preceding action has been realistic—there is no reason why the denouement should be. After the action has been worked out to an impasse, the playwright gaily admits that this is art, not life, and quickly straightens things out with a courtier's bow to his own *deus ex machina,* Louis XIV.

Thus the Anglo-Saxon reader finds himself confronted by a strange and foreign set of theatrical conventions. Let him reflect, however, that he accepts without question all manner of supernatural events and improbable denouements in Shakespeare. Those who would object to lawyer Portia, say, would be quite properly told that in the theater one is willing to suspend one's disbelief. Let us grant the same tolerance to Molière, and realize that insofar as *characterization* and *unity of tone* are concerned his solution is the most coherent one possible. Let us further respect the statement of the great actor-director Louis Jouvet that in the theater Molière's denouements work.

IV

As *Tartuffe* may be seen as a symbol of the short-lived triumph of secularism at the court of Louis XIV, so too its subject matter and the battles waged against it may be viewed in a larger ideological context. *Tartuffe* may stand as the symbol of one of the most important contributions of seventeenth-century France to the history of ideas—the distinction between intention and act, between the psychological roots of an action and the outer face of the action itself. The name of La Rochefoucauld, of course, springs most immediately to mind in this context, but the sudden, painfully fresh awareness of this possibility of distinction informs the writing of many other great names in this century: Jean Racine, Cardinal de Retz, Mme de Sévigné, La Fontaine, La Bruyère, to name a few.[3] One may see the growth of the "modern spirit" in the

[3] François, duc de la Rochefoucauld (1613–1680), author of the *Maximes,* in which he proposed that our acts are so subtly intertwined with our self-interest that we ourselves are unaware of our true motives.

increasing attention paid to this distinction, from medieval Christians at one pole to disciples of Freud at the opposite pole. In the Middle Ages the deed stood for itself, spoke for itself, was itself, was important for its own sake. The dominant literary form, the *chansons de geste,* told of deeds *(gesta).* This is not to say that hypocrisy was unknown, that the slyness of Renart went unnoticed, but rather to insist that public acts had more forcefulness, more efficacy, were invested with a more sacred, sacramental nature than they are today. Whatever his motives, the penance of Henry IV at Canossa carried its own weight in the act itself.[4] Processions, pilgrimages, *sacres*—religious acts and attitudes in general—had an unquestioned reality which they have lost in proportion to the concurrent progress of secularization and psychological probing. In this process, the contribution of seventeenth-century France was crucial.

The questions concerning the relationship between illusion and reality, and their analogues, appearance and truth, charlatanism and deed, intention and act, hypocrisy and sincerity, were not invented by Pirandello in the twentieth century; Boccaccio knew them; the author of *The Life of Lazarillo de Tormes* knew them, as did Cervantes and Montaigne. These problems, which are vital in the life of genius, are especially urgent in the life of the theater. *Othello, L'Illusion comique,*

Jean Racine (1639–1699), the greatest of all French writers of tragedy. In his plays duty usually serves as a pretext for private motives.

Cardinal de Retz (1613–1679), leader of intrigues in the civil disturbances in the middle of the century. Author of brilliantly penetrating *Mémoires.*

Madame de Sévigné (1626–1696), author of several volumes of letters posthumously published. She, too, penetrated behind the façade which the courtiers offered to the public.

Jean de la Fontaine (1621–1695), author of the famous *Fables.* His characters unwittingly reveal egocentric motives behind their fine words.

Jean de la Bruyère (1645–1696). His *Caractères* act with humility or pride according to their social station.

[4] Henry IV (*ca.* 1050–1106), Holy Roman Emperor from 1056 to 1106. Carried on a long struggle with Pope Gregory VII, who excommunicated him after the Diet of Worms. Abandoned by his partisans, Henry dressed himself in penitent's garb and knelt in the snow before Gregory's palace at Canossa for four months until the Pope was forced to give in.

Faust, Part II, bear ample witness. These questions came to a focus of unequaled intensity in seventeenth-century France, and more particularly in a series of three of Molière's greatest plays: *Le Tartuffe* (1664); *Dom Juan* (1665), in which the hypocritical but likeable seducer ends up as a religious hypocrite as well; and *Le Misanthrope* (1666), in which the "hero" goes to the opposite extreme of practicing—or trying to practice—total sincerity in *salon* society. Molière takes both sides; he does not give us pat answers, just as his denouements, being particular and local, do not answer the problems of the plot, but he does pose questions that can be as troubling today as they were in his time.

Viewed in this context many facets of *Tartuffe* and its history reacquire sense. The Church faction was perfectly correct from its own point of view in considering this play subversive, for it strikes directly at the sacramental nature of religious acts —that is, the correspondence between the outward and visible sign and the inward and spiritual grace. Furthermore, at this point in history, the words of Louis' edict are not out of line with good sense when they say that some unenlightened people might not make the proper distinctions between the false and the true. Our awareness of these facts helps us to recapture the sense of Cléante's impassioned and lengthy pleas that the distinction between true and false piety must be made.

V

The translation tries to avoid the use of pseudoarchaic "translator's English," without falling into an equally false American colloquialism. Departing even more radically from tradition, it adheres to no fixed form, despite the fact that Molière's original is written entirely in rhyming Alexandrine couplets. In this translation, Cléante's reasonableness is rendered in prose, Dorine's wit in doggerel, Tartuffe's passion in verse. In all but a few instances, where I felt that accurate rendering of emotion was of primary importance, the translation may be said to be literal. In short, I tried to replace the xx • T<small>ARTUFFE</small>

outward adherence to form by an inner, and I think more important, fidelity to the tone and contours of Molière's original.

An earlier version of this translation was performed May 6–18, 1954, by the Princeton University Theatre Intime and published in A. S. Downer's *The Art of the Play* (New York: Henry Holt and Co., 1955). The present version has been completely reworked for The Library of Liberal Arts.

R<small>OBERT</small> W. H<small>ARTLE</small>

Chronology of Molière's Life

1622 Baptism in Paris of Jean-Baptiste Poquelin, eldest son of Jean Poquelin, upholsterer by appointment to the king

1632 Death of Molière's mother

1632?–1639? Studies at the Collège de Clermont, Paris

1640? Studies law

1642 Assumes some of his father's duties during a court visit to Narbonne

1643 Renounces succession to his father's post

With Madeleine Béjart and other actors, forms the "Illustre-Théâtre"

The "Illustre-Théâtre" plays in Rouen

1644 Debut of the "Illustre-Théâtre" in Paris

Takes the name "Molière." Named leader of the troupe

1645 Failure of the "Illustre-Théâtre"

Imprisoned for debts

1645–1658 Freed from prison. The "Illustre-Théâtre" travels in the provinces

1658 Molière's troupe performs at court Corneille's *Nicomède* and a farce by Molière

Installed in Paris under the nominal patronage of the king's brother

1659 *Les Précieuses ridicules* (*The Precious Young Ladies*)

1660 *Sganarelle ou le Cocu imaginaire* (*Sganarelle, or the Imaginary Cuckold*)

1661 *Dom Garcie de Navarre*, Molière's first and last attempt at tragicomedy.

L'Ecole des Maris (*The School for Husbands*)

Les Fâcheux (*The Bores*), first presented at Fouquet's castle before the king, just before the former's arrest

1662   Marriage of Molière and Armande Béjart, the younger
       sister (some contemporaries said the daughter) of
       Madeleine Béjart, his former mistress.
       L'Ecole des Femmes (*The School for Wives*)
1663   Receives an allowance of a thousand *livres* from the
       king
       Replies to violent criticism of *The School for Wives*
       with two short, witty counterattacks in dramatic form
1664   Birth, baptism (with the king as godfather), and death
       of first child, Louis
       Le Tartuffe
       Molière's troupe plays Racine's first tragedy, *La
       Thébaïde*
1665   *Dom Juan*
       Birth of Molière's daughter
       The troupe becomes officially "The King's Troupe";
       Molière's allowance is raised to six thousand *livres.*
       Molière's troupe performs Racine's *Alexandre.* Racine
       secretly gives the play to a rival troupe. Quarrel and
       rupture in relations between the two
1666   *Le Misanthrope*
       Le Médecin malgré lui (*The Doctor in Spite of Him-
       self*)
1667   *The Impostor,* closed down after one performance
1668   *Amphitryon*
       George Dandin
       L'Avare (*The Miser*)
1670   *Le Bourgeois gentilhomme* (*The Would-Be Gentleman*)
1671   *Les Fourberies de Scapin* (*Scapin's Sharp Tricks*)
1672   Death of Madeleine Béjart
       Les Femmes savantes (*The Learned Ladies*)
       Birth of Molière's third child, who dies within a few
       weeks
1673   February 10: *Première* of *Le Malade Imaginaire* (*The
       Imaginary Invalid*)
       February 17: During fourth performance, Molière, play-

ing the "Invalid," taken violently ill, carried home, where he dies without benefit of clergy

February 21: Molière buried at night without religious services [1]

1680 The remainder of Molière's troupe, plus two others, joined by royal order to become "The King's Troupe," the ancestor of today's Comédie Française

[1] At the time actors were automatically excommunicated until such time as they repented, confessed, and left the profession. Often this change of heart occurred in their death agony. Molière died too rapidly, thus dying excommunicate.

Selected Bibliography

The text of *Le Tartuffe* used for the present translation is found in Molière, *Œuvres*, edited by Despois and Mesnard, "Collection les Grand Écrivains de la France" (Paris: Hatchette, 1873–1900).

The reader may wish to consult the following works in English:

CAIRNCROSS, JOHN. *New Light on Molière*. Geneva: Droz, 1956. —A clear and easily read discussion of the questions surrounding the first versions of *Tartuffe*.

GOSSMAN, LIONEL. *Men and Masks: A Study of Molière*. Baltimore: The Johns Hopkins University Press, 1963.—A good chapter on *Tartuffe* stresses the importance of Orgon's role.

HARVEY, SIR PAUL, and HESELTINE, J. E. *The Oxford Companion to French Literature*. Oxford: Oxford University Press, 1959.—A useful and well-written dictionary of French literature.

HUBERT, JUDD D. *Molière and the Comedy of the Intellect*. Berkeley: The University of California Press, 1962.—Subtle textual analysis.

LANCASTER, HENRY C. *A History of French Dramatic Literature in the Seventeenth Century*. 9 vols. Baltimore: The Johns Hopkins University Press, 1929–1942.—Detailed but well indexed.

MOORE, W. G. *Molière: A New Criticism*. Oxford: Oxford University Press, 1949.—By far the best book on Molière in English.

TARTUFFE

First Petition

PRESENTED TO THE KING

Concerning the Comedy Tartuffe

SIRE,

Whereas the duty of comedy is to correct men by amusing them, I felt that, being in that profession, I could do no better than to attack by ludicrous portrayals the vices of my age; and since hypocrisy is certainly one of the commonest, most disagreeable, and most dangerous, the thought occurred to me, Sire, that I should render no small service to all the upstanding people of your kingdom, if I wrote a comedy which would discredit hypocrites and properly expose all the studied grimaces of those excessively pious folk, all the covert rascalities of those counterfeits of piety who try to trap men with spurious zeal and sophistical charity.

I made this comedy, Sire, with, I believe, all the possible care and circumspection demanded by the delicate nature of the subject; and, the better to preserve the esteem and respect we owe to the truly pious, I differentiated as well as I could between them and the character I had to deal with. I have left no ambiguity, I have removed whatever could confuse good with evil, and in this portrait I have used only clear colors and essential traits that make immediately manifest a true, out-and-out hypocrite.

Nevertheless, all my precautions have come to naught. They took advantage, Sire, of the susceptibility of your heart in matters of religion, and they were able to overcome you in the only way by which you are vulnerable, I mean by your respect for sacred things. The tartuffes have had the underhanded skill to find grace in the eyes of your Majesty; in short, the originals have had the copy suppressed, no matter how innocent nor how true the likeness.

Although the suppression of this work was a severe blow, nevertheless my misfortune was softened by your Majesty's explanation of this matter; and I believed, Sire, that you relieved me of all grounds for complaint by your kindness in saying that your Majesty found nothing to criticize in the play that you forbade me to present in public.

But despite this splendorous declaration from the greatest as well as the most enlightened king in the world, despite the added approval of his Eminence the Papal Legate [1] and the great majority of our prelates, who all, after my private readings of the work, have been in agreement with the sentiments of your Majesty; despite all that, I say, we see a book composed by the curate of ——[2] which brazenly contradicts all that august testimony. Your Majesty speaks for nothing, and his Eminence the Legate and the prelates give judgment for nothing; my comedy—though not seen—is diabolical, and diabolical, my brain; I am a devil dressed in flesh and clothed like a man, a freethinker, impious, worthy of an exemplary execution. Public burning would not suffice to expiate my offense, that would be letting me off too lightly; this worthy gentleman is careful not to stop there in his charitable zeal: he wants me to get no mercy from God; he insists that I be damned—the matter is settled.

This book, Sire, was presented to your Majesty; and, surely, you can imagine how disagreeable it is for me to be exposed every day to those gentlemen's insults, how much wrong such calumnies will do me in the world if they must be tolerated, and, finally, how much it is in my interest to be purged of its deceit and to make known to the public that my comedy is

1 The Papal Legate, Cardinal Chigi, nephew of Pope Alexander VII and his ambassador extraordinary, had heard a reading of *Tartuffe* while at Fontainebleau.

2 A certain Pierre Roullé, curate of Saint-Barthélemy, had published a vitriolic pamphlet against Molière. The expressions used by Molière are taken directly from this work. As a result of Molière's petition, Roullé was made to feel that his work of supererogation was not appreciated.

nothing like what is claimed. I shall not say, Sire, what I should like to request for my reputation and to justify to all the innocence of my work. Enlightened kings like yourself have no need to have our wishes pointed out; they see, like God, what we need, and know better than we what they should grant to us. It is sufficient to place my interests in the hands of your Majesty and to await respectfully whatever it may please your Majesty to ordain.

Second Petition

PRESENTED TO THE KING

In his camp before the city of Lille in Flanders, by La Thorillière and La Grange,[3] actors of his Majesty's troupe and colleagues of Monsieur Molière, concerning the interdict that was laid the sixth of August, 1667, on the presentation of Tartuffe *until further ordered by his Majesty.*

SIRE,

It is a piece of great temerity on my part to come and importune a great monarch in the midst of his glorious conquests, but in my present state where, Sire, can I find protection save in the place where I seek it? And to whom can I make solicitation against the authority of a power that crushes me, save to the source of power and authority, the just dispenser of absolute orders, the sovereign judge and master of all things?

My comedy, Sire, was not able to enjoy the kindness of your Majesty. For naught I presented it under the title of *The Impostor* and disguised the character under the trappings of a man of the world; in vain I gave him a little hat, long hair, a wide collar, a sword, and lace all over his costume, softened several places and carefully eliminated everything that I thought could give the slightest shadow of a pretext to the famous original models of the portrait I wished to make; all

---

3 Before leaving to take personal command of his armies in Flanders, Louis XIV had apparently given Molière verbal permission to present his revised version of the play. After the first performance, the police forbade its further presentation. The order came from Guillaume de Lamoignon, First President of the Paris *parlement*, who, unbeknownst to Molière, was a member of the Company of the Holy Sacrament.

6

that was of no use. The cabal awoke upon the mere conjectures that they could make about the affair. They found means to catch by surprise minds that, on any other subject, are proud of not being able to be taken unawares. My comedy had no sooner appeared than it was struck by a bolt from a power that must command respect; and all that I could do, in those circumstances, to save my own self in this bursting storm was to say that your Majesty had had the kindness to permit the presentation and that I had not thought it necessary to ask permission of others, since it was your Majesty alone who had forbidden it.

I do not doubt, Sire, that the folk whom I depict in my comedy are trying to use influence with your Majesty, nor that they are thrusting onto their side—as they have already done —truly upright people, who are all the more easily fooled because they judge others by themselves. They [the hypocrites] have the art of daubing fine colors over all their intentions. Whatever semblance they wear, it is not at all God's interest that moves them; they have proved it enough by the comedies they have allowed to be presented so many times in public without their saying the slightest word. They do so because the latter merely attacked piety and religion, about which they care very little, but this one attacks *them* and makes sport of them personally; and that is what they cannot stand. They cannot forgive me for unveiling their impostures for all to see; and they will certainly not fail to tell your Majesty that everyone is scandalized by my comedy. But the pure truth, Sire, is that all Paris is scandalized only by the interdict, that the most scrupulous found its presentation profitable, and that there is astonishment that people of such known probity should have such great deference for people who should be regarded with horror by everyone and who are so opposed to the true piety which they profess.

I await with respect the judgment which your Majesty will deign to pronounce on this matter, but it is very certain, Sire, that I must no longer think of making comedies if the tartuffes have the upper hand; for they will feel authorized thereby to persecute me more than ever and will try to censure the most innocent things that may come from my pen.

May your kindness, Sire, give me protection against their poisoned slander; and may I, upon your return from such a glorious campaign, ease your Majesty from the fatigues of his conquests, give him innocent pleasure after such noble labors, and give laughter to the monarch who gives tremors to all Europe!

Third Petition

PRESENTED TO THE KING

The fifth of February, 1669

SIRE,

A very honest doctor,[4] whose patient I have the honor to be, promises me, and is willing to swear to it before a notary, that he will make me live another thirty years if I can obtain a favor from your Majesty. About his promise I told him that I did not ask so much, and that I should be satisfied if he would swear not to kill me. The favor, Sire, is a canonicate in your royal chapel of Vincennes, vacant since the death of ——.

Do I dare ask this additional favor of your Majesty the very day of the great resurrection of *Tartuffe,* brought to life by your kindness? I am, by that first favor, reconciled with the devout; and I would, by the second one, be reconciled with the doctors.[5] This is certainly too many favors at once for me, but perhaps it is not too many for your Majesty, and I await, with a little respectful hope, the answer to my petition.

[4] A certain Monsieur de Mauvillain.—Note the tone of confident joy and almost of camaraderie.

[5] Molière had made sport of doctors in *Dom Juan, Doctor Love,* and *The Doctor in Spite of Himself.*

Preface

Here is a comedy about which people have raised quite a stir, which has long been persecuted, and the people it mocks have made plain that they were more powerful in France than all those I have mocked heretofore. The marquises, the precious ladies, the cuckolds, and the doctors have suffered the portrayal in peace, and have even made a show of being amused, like everyone else, by the sketches we made of them. But the hypocrites could not take mockery; they were immediately affrighted, and found it strange that I should be so bold as to make sport of their grimacing and wish to criticize an occupation meddled in by so many honest folk. It is a crime they could not forgive, and they all took up arms against my comedy with a frightful furor. They were careful not to attack it through the side that hurt them—they are too politic for that, and know too well how to get along in the world to unveil the depths of their soul. Following their praiseworthy custom, they concealed their private interests with the cause of God, and in their words *Tartuffe* is a play that offends religion. From one end to the other it is full of abominations, and there is nothing in it that does not deserve the flames. All its syllables are impious; even the gestures are criminal; and the slightest glance, the slightest shake of the head, the slightest step to left or right hide mysteries which they manage to explain to my disadvantage.

In vain I have submitted it to my friends' judgment and to everybody's censure; the corrections I have been able to make, the judgment of the king and queen, who have seen it, the approval of the great princes and ministers, who have publicly honored it with their presence, the testimony of upright people, who found it useful—all that has not helped at all. They will not let go; and every day, still, they prompt the public outcry of indiscreet zealots, who insult me piously and damn me from charity.

I should care very little about anything they can say, were it not for the artifice by which they create for me enemies whom I respect, and thrust onto their side truly worthy people, whose good faith they catch unawares, and who in their enthusiasm for Heaven's best interests are easily impressionable. That is what obliges me to defend myself. It is to the truly pious that I wish everywhere to justify myself about the conduct of my comedy; and I beseech them with all my heart not to condemn things before seeing them, to rid themselves of all prejudice, and not to serve the passion of those whose grimacing dishonors them.

If one takes the trouble to examine my comedy in good faith, one will see without a doubt that my intentions throughout are innocent and that it in nowise tends to make sport of things that we must revere; that I have treated it with all the precautions required by the delicate nature of the subject and that I have put all the art and all the care possible to distinguish clearly between the character who is the hypocrite and the one who is truly devout. To that end, I have used two whole acts to prepare the arrival of my scoundrel. He does not keep the spectator in suspense for a single moment; he is recognized immediately by the characteristics that I give him; and, from one end to the other, he does not say a word, he does not do one action, that does not depict for the spectators the character of a wicked man or enhance the character of the truly upright man whom I place next to him as a foil.

Of course I know that in reply those gentlemen try to insinuate that it is not up to the theater to speak of these subjects, but I beg leave to ask them on what basis they establish this fine maxim. This is merely a hypothetical premise, which they in nowise prove; and it would present absolutely no difficulty to point out to them that ancient drama had its origins in religion and was a part of their mysteries; that our neighbors, the Spaniards, mingle drama into the celebration of practically all their holy days, and that even with us the theater owes its birth to the cares of a confraternity that today still owns the Hôtel de Bourgogne; [1] that it is a place that was given for the presentation of the most important mysteries of our faith; that one can still see plays printed in gothic type under the name of a Sorbonne doctor,[2] and, without going so far afield, that in our own time Monsieur de Corneille's religious plays were produced and were admired by all of France.[3]

If the mission of comedy is to correct men's vices, I fail to see why some should be privileged. In the State, this one is of an importance much more dangerous than all the others; and we have seen that the theater is a great force for correction. The finest points of a serious morality are usually less powerful than those belonging to satire; and most men are scolded by nothing quite so well as by the portrayal of their faults. It is a great blow to vice to expose it to everyone's laughter. We can easily stand being reprehended, but we cannot stand being mocked. We are willing to be wicked, but we will not be ridiculous.

I have been reproached for having placed terms of piety in the mouth of my impostor. Well! Could I help it in properly representing the character of a hypocrite? To me, it seems enough for me to make known the criminal motives that make him say those things, and for me to have cut out sacred terms, for it would have been repugnant to hear him make bad usage of them.—"But in the fourth act he propounds a pernicious morality."—But is not this morality something we have heard about over and over again?[4] Does it say anything new in my comedy? And can it be feared that things so widely

---

[1] The Hôtel de Bourgogne, where the Royal Troupe played, was owned by the Confraternity of the Passion and Resurrection of Our Lord. From 1402 to 1548, this group enjoyed the exclusive right to perform mystery plays in Paris.

[2] Molière refers to a passion play edited by Jehan Michel, doctor of *medicine*. He has confused him with a theologian of the same name.

[3] *Polyeucte*, one of Corneille's greatest plays, and *Théodore, Virgin and Martyr.*

[4] In Pascal's *Provincial Letters.*

detested should have any influence over people's minds, or that they should gain authority in the mouth of a scoundrel? There is no probability in that; and the comedy *Tartuffe* should be approved, or else all comedies condemned.

And that is precisely what has recently been raging, and never have some people been so furious against the theater. I cannot deny that there have been Fathers of the Church who condemned the drama, but no one can deny that there have also been some who treated it a little more gently. Thus, the authority on which the proposed censure is based is destroyed by this division, and the only conclusion that can be drawn from this diversity of opinions in minds enlightened by the same intelligence is that they have considered the drama differently, and that some have taken it in its pure state while the others have looked at its corruption and have confused it with those base spectacles which have been correctly called "spectacles of turpitude." [5]

And indeed, since one should discourse on things and not words, and since most contradictions come from lack of understanding and from wrapping up contrary things in the same word, one need merely lift the veil of equivocation and look at what comedy is per se to see whether it is reprehensible. It will be agreed, no doubt, that, being nothing other than a skillful poem which, by agreeable lessons, reprimands men's defects, it could not be censured save unjustly; and, if we wish to hear the witness of antiquity on this matter, she will tell us that her most famous philosophers praised comedy, they who professed such austere restraint and who incessantly cried out against the vices of their age. She will point out to us that Aristotle consecrated his night watches to the drama and took the trouble of reducing the art of making comedies to precepts.[6] She will teach us that her greatest and highest ranking men gloried in composing some themselves,[7] that there were

---

[5] The expression is St. Augustine's.

[6] In the seventeenth century, the word *comédie* could mean "comedy," "drama," "theater," or even "tragedy."

[7] Scipio's collaboration with Terence.

others who did not scorn to recite in public those which they
had composed; that Greece manifested her esteem for this art
by the glorious prizes and the splendid theaters with which
she did it honor; and that in Rome itself this same art also received extraordinary honors. I do not mean in Rome debauched under licentious emperors, but in Rome disciplined
under austere consuls, in the time of vigorous Roman virtue.[8]

I admit that there have been times when comedy was corrupt. But what is there in the world that is not corrupted
every day? There is nothing so innocent that men cannot stain
it with crime, no art so salutary that they cannot reverse its
intentions, nothing so good in itself that they cannot turn it
to bad uses. Medicine is a beneficial art and everyone respects
it as one of the most excellent things we have, yet there have
been times when it became odious and often it has been made
into an art for poisoning men. Philosophy is a gift of Heaven;
it was given to us to lead our minds to the knowledge of God
through contemplating the miracles of nature; nevertheless,
everyone is aware that it has often been perverted from its
function and publicly used to uphold impiety. Even the holiest
of things are not safe from men's corrupting, and we see
scoundrels who every day abuse piety and wickedly make it
serve the greatest crimes. But for all of that one does not fail
to make the necessary distinctions. One does not bundle together into one false conclusion the true excellence of the
things being corrupted and the malice of the corruptors. One
goes on separating the bad usage from the goal of the art, and
just as we do not take it into our heads to forbid medicine because it was banished from Rome,[9] or philosophy because it
was publicly condemned in Athens,[10] likewise we should not
wish to interdict comedy because it has been criticized at cer-

[8] Molière is contrasting the legendary civic virtue of Rome under the
Republic with the public debauchery of emperors such as Claudius, Nero,
and others. Both Plautus and Terence lived and wrote during the days
of the Republic.
[9] Pliny, *Natural History* XXIX. 8.
[10] In the person of Socrates.

tain times. That censure had its reasons, which do not exist today. It was restricted to what it could see, and we must not draw it out beyond its own self-appointed limits, nor stretch it further than is right, and make it embrace the innocent with the guilty. The comedy it aimed to attack is not the one that we would defend. One must be careful not to confuse the one with the other. They are two persons whose manners and morals are completely opposite. They have no connection with each other beyond the similarity of the name; and it would be a frightful injustice to want to condemn Olympe, who is an upright woman, because there is an Olympe who was depraved. Judgments like that would perforce cause a great disorder in the world. By that system everything would be condemned; and since we do not hold that severity against so many things that are abused every day, we should then grant the same grace to comedy and approve plays wherein we see instruction and propriety reign.

I know that there are some souls who are so dainty that they cannot suffer any comedy, who say that the most proper are the most dangerous, that the passions depicted are all the more touching in that they are filled with virtue, and that souls are moved to tenderness by those kinds of representations. I cannot see that it is such a great crime to be moved at the sight of a chaste passion, and it is a high plane of virtue, that complete insensitivity to which they would lift up our soul. I doubt that such a perfection lies within the strength of human nature, and I do not know whether it is not better to work at rectifying and tempering men's passions rather than trying to do away with them altogether. I admit that there are better places to frequent than the theater; and if we are going to reprove all the things that do not directly concern God and our salvation, it is certain that comedy must be among them, and I find no fault at its being condemned with the rest; but if we allow, as is true, that the exercises of piety suffer intervals and that men need diversion, I maintain that they cannot find a more innocent one than comedy. But this has been too protracted. Let us finish with a *mot* from a great prince about the comedy *Tartuffe*.[11]

A week after it was forbidden, a play called *Hermit Scaramouche* was presented before the court; [12] on leaving, the king said to this great prince, "I should really like to know why the people who are so scandalized about Molière's comedy don't say a word about *Scaramouche*." To which the prince replied, "The reason is that the comedy *Scaramouche* makes sport of Heaven and religion, which those gentlemen don't care a hang about, but Molière's comedy makes sport of *them*, which is what they cannot stand."

[11] The Prince de Condé, a prince of the blood belonging to a collateral line of the House of Bourbon, was the commander responsible for many great victories of the time. Condé was a champion of *Tartuffe*.

[12] A licentious play about a debauched monk who frequently "mortified the flesh."

Characters

MADAME PERNELLE, mother of ORGON
ORGON, ELMIRE's husband
ELMIRE, ORGON's wife
DAMIS, ORGON's son
MARIANE, ORGON's daughter, in love with VALÈRE
VALÈRE, MARIANE's sweetheart
CLÉANTE, ORGON's brother-in-law
TARTUFFE, religious hypocrite [1]
DORINE, lady's maid to MARIANE
MONSIEUR LOYAL, Justice of the Peace
AN OFFICER OF THE CROWN
FLIPOTE, MME PERNELLE's servant

THE SCENE: *Paris, a room in the house of* ORGON. *A door at each side and a raised entrance at the back. Downstage right, a small door leading into a tiny room. A table covered with a great cloth; chairs.*[2]

[1] The origin of the name "Tartuffe" is obscure. Some ten years previously, the hero of Scarron's novel, *Les Hypocrites*, was called "Montufar"; perhaps he suggested to Molière Tartuffe's costume, false modesty, and gluttony. Whatever the source, the word *tartuffe* quickly gained acceptance and, scarcely thirty years later, was admitted to the first edition of the French Academy's dictionary as a common noun meaning a religious hypocrite.

[2] The scene remains the same throughout the play, in accordance with a French tradition, or "rule," dating back about thirty years. Mairet introduced the "Rule of the Three Unities," that is, the doctrine that a play

should consist of one main action, represented as occurring at one time (i.e., in one day or less), at one place. This doctrine was supposed to be based on Aristotle's *Poetics,* although in fact Aristotle speaks only of unity of time. (See Paul Harvey and J. E. Heseltine, *The Oxford Companion to French Literature,* s.v. "Tragedy.") From Molière's observance of these rules, as well as his use of the five-act format and alexandrine verse, we may infer the high seriousness of his purpose.

It is worth noting the suppleness with which Molière motivates exits and entrances.

A few of the stage directions are Molière's, but most have been added by the translator in conformity with the traditional staging at the Comédie Française.

Act One

(I. 1) [1]

(*Enter right,* MME PERNELLE, *pushing* FLIPOTE *ahead of her with her cane.* ELMIRE, MARIANE, DORINE, DAMIS, *and* CLÉANTE *follow.* MME PERNELLE *limps badly but moves along with determination and speed.*)

MME PERNELLE: Come on, Flipote, come on, let me get away from them.

ELMIRE: It's hard to follow you at such a pace.

MME PERNELLE: Never mind, my dear daughter-in-law, never mind; don't come any farther; those are airs you don't need for me.

ELMIRE: What you deserve you shall receive in full. But why are you leaving so quickly, Mother?

MME PERNELLE: Because I can't look at such a household and, as for pleasing me, no one takes any thought. Yes, I'm leaving your house quite scandalized; all my advice is contradicted; nothing is sacred, everyone shouts, and it is a perfect Court of Fools.

DORINE: If . . .

MME PERNELLE: You, dearie, are a serving-girl who's a little too loud in the mouth and very impertinent; you butt in to give your advice about everything.[2]

---

[1] French convention marks a new "scene" each time an actor enters or leaves the stage. Actually, the curtain does not go down nor does the scenery change. In this translation, it has been thought preferable to indicate entrances and exits in the usual English manner and to print the French act and scene numbers in the margin.

[2] *Tartuffe* displays a finely nuanced conflict between two different milieux. Madame Pernelle and her son Orgon come from a lower level on the social scale than do Elmire and Cléante. Madame Pernelle's language is earthy, filled with proverbs and folk wisdom. She mistrusts the superior dress and sophistication of Elmire and Cléante. She, Orgon, and Monsieur

19

DAMIS: But . . .

MME PERNELLE: You are a fool, my boy—*f-o-o-l;* I'm the one who's telling you so and I'm your grandmother. I have warned my son, your father, a hundred times that you were turning out to be a good-for-nothing, and would never give him anything but trouble.

MARIANE: I think . . .

MME PERNELLE: And his sister . . . heavens! You play the quiet one, and you're so innocent and sweetie-sweet, but, just as they say, still waters run deep, and you carry on something sly that I detest.

ELMIRE: But, Mother . . .

MME PERNELLE: If you don't mind my saying so, dear daughter-in-law, your behavior is altogether bad; you ought to set them a good example, and their late mother managed much better. You're loose with your money, and it offends me to see you decked out like a princess. Whoever wants to please her husband only, dear daughter-in-law, does not need so much finery.

CLÉANTE: But Madame, after all . . .

MME PERNELLE: As for her brother, sir, I respect you greatly, love and revere you; but if I were my son, her husband, I would strongly beg you not to enter our house. You are forever preaching rules of life that no decent person ought to follow. I'm speaking a little frankly to you, but that's the way I am; when something rankles in me I don't mince words.

DAMIS: Your Monsieur Tartuffe is perfect, I suppose.

MME PERNELLE: He is a good man who must be listened to, and I can't help getting angry to see him disputed by a fool like you.

DAMIS: What! Am I supposed to allow a nagging bigot to come into this house and usurp tyrannical power, so that we can't amuse ourselves in any way if *that (points to* TARTUFFE'S *door)* fine gentleman does not deign to consent?

Loyal address Dorine as *mamie,* which I have rendered as "dearie." Later she threatens to box Flipote's ears and calls her *gaupe,* "slut."

DORINE: If you're supposed to listen to him and believe his maxims, you can't do anything without committing a crime, because that fanatical critic condemns everything.

MME PERNELLE: And everything he condemns is very well condemned. It's the road to heaven he wants to lead you on, and my son's example ought to bring you all to love him.

DAMIS: Now look, Mother, there's no father, or anyone else, who can force me to wish him well. I would betray my own heart if I said anything else; his way of acting makes me lose my temper every time; I can see the end of it: that lout and I will have some kind of fine explosion.

DORINE: Yes, and it's a scandalous thing to see a stranger set himself up in this house—a beggar, who didn't have any shoes when he came, and whose whole suit wasn't worth six cents, should so far forget himself as to interfere with everything and play the master.

MME PERNELLE: Oh! Lord love me! Everything would be much better off if all were governed by his pious commands.

DORINE: He passes for a saint in your fancy; his whole conduct—believe me—is nothing but hypocrisy.

MME PERNELLE: Listen to that chatter!

DORINE: I wouldn't trust him any more than I would his Laurent, without a good guarantee.

MME PERNELLE: I don't know what the servant may be underneath, but I guarantee the master for a good man. The only reason you wish him ill and snub him is that he tells you all the truth about yourselves. His heart is stirred to anger against sin, and heaven's cause is all that moves him.

DORINE: Yes; but why, especially lately, can't he stand for anyone to hang around the house? How does a decent visit offend heaven so that he has to kick up a row that'd drive you crazy? Do you want me to tell you my opinion—just among ourselves? I think it's over Madame (*indicating* ELMIRE), and that he's just plain jealous.

MME PERNELLE: Hush up and think what you're saying.

He's not the only one who blames those visits. All that hubbub that follows the people you associate with, those carriages always parked at the door and the noisy crowd of lackeys make an unpleasant uproar in the whole neighborhood. I'm willing to believe that there's really nothing to it, but people *are* talking about it and that isn't good.

CLÉANTE: Come, come, Madame, do you want to stop people from talking? It would be an unfortunate thing in life if, on account of the stupid way people can talk, one had to give up one's best friends; and, even if you could bring yourself to do it, would you expect to impose silence on everyone? Against slander there are no ramparts. So let us pay no attention to all the silly cackle; let us make every effort to live in all innocence and let the gossips go their way.

DORINE: Daphne, our neighbor, and her little husband, aren't they the ones who talk about us?

> Those whose behavior is most open to laughter
> Are always the first to heap on the slander.

They never fail to leap on the slightest glimmer of an inclination, publish the news with great glee, and give it the twist they want it to take. By tinting other people's actions with *their* colors, they think they can justify their own in the eyes of the world, and, with the false hope of some similarity, lend an innocence to their *real* intrigues, or scatter elsewhere some of the arrows of public blame that overwhelm them.

MME PERNELLE: All those arguments have nothing to do with the case. It is well known that Orante leads an exemplary life; all her thoughts are directed toward heaven; and I have learned through some people that she highly disapproves of the crowd that comes to this house.

DORINE: That's a wonderful example! She is a good lady! It is true that she leads an austere life, but age has put that burning zeal in her soul and everyone knows that she is a prude through physical necessity. As long as she could attract amorous attentions she made full use of her advantages; but, seeing the lights dim in her eyes, now that the world is passing her by, she wants to renounce it and, with the high and mighty veil of a lofty virtue, disguise the weakness of her outworn charms. Those are the tricks of yesterday's coquettes. It's hard on them to be deserted by their gentlemen-in-waiting. In such neglect, their gloomy anxiety sees no other way out but to trade on prudery. The severity of these upright ladies censures everything and pardons nothing. Loudly they criticize everyone's life—not for charity's sake but because their barbed envy can't stand for anyone else to enjoy the pleasures from which declining age has weaned their desires.[3]

MME PERNELLE: That's the kind of bedtime stories it takes to please you. My dear daughter-in-law, one is forced to keep silence in your house, for Madame (*indicating* DORINE) holds the floor all day long with her chattering; but just the same I intend to take my turn at speaking out.—I tell you that my son never did anything wiser than taking in that devout person; that heaven sent him to this house in time of need to put all your souls back on the right track; that you must listen to him for your own salvation, and that he doesn't reprimand anything that doesn't need reprimanding. These visits, these fancy balls, these little chats are all inventions of the Evil One. Here a pious word is never heard; it's all idle tales, nonsense and foolishness; very often one's neighbor gets his, and you know how to slander first one and then the other. Anyway, the uproar from such gatherings makes sensible people's heads spin; a thousand cacklings start up in a flash, and, as a preacher said very well the other day, it's a real tower of Babylon, where all the people babble on; and the story he went on to tell . . . (*Pointing to* CLÉANTE) Isn't that Monsieur snickering already? Go find your own crowd of fools that make you laugh, and without . . . Farewell, daughter-in-law, I won't say another word, but let me tell you that my opinion of this household has gone down fifty per cent, and it'll be many a day before I set foot in it again. (*Giving* FLIPOTE *a slap.*)

---

[3] According to the *Letter on the Impostor*, in 1667 most of this speech was spoken by Cléante; this may account for its being in a more elevated style than what we would expect from Dorine.

Come on, you, quit dreaming there with your mouth hanging open. By God, I'll box your ears! Forward, slut, forward!

(I. 2)   *(Exeunt left all but* CLÉANTE *and* DORINE.*)*

CLÉANTE: I don't want to go along for fear she might scold me again. How that dear old lady . . .

DORINE: Ah! Goodness! It's too bad she didn't hear you say that; she'd tell you right enough that you're very kind but she isn't *that* old.

CLÉANTE: How excited she got over nothing! She seems to be completely crazy over her Tartuffe.

DORINE: Oh, really, all that is nothing compared with her son; and if you had seen him, you would say it's even worse. The civil wars had set him up as a sensible man, and he showed courage in serving his king,[4] but he's been like a man out of his senses ever since he became infatuated with Tartuffe. He calls him his brother and loves him in spirit a hundred times more than he does mother, son, wife, and daughter. He makes him sole confidant of all his secrets and the prudent director of his actions. He pets him and embraces him; I don't think you could have more affection for a mistress; at table he wants him to sit in the place of honor, and joyously sees him eat enough for six; he makes everyone give him the choicest morsels; and, if Tartuffe should happen to belch, he says, "God bless you!"[5] All in all, he is crazy about him; Tartuffe is his all, his hero, he admires him all the time, quotes him on every occasion, thinks his slightest actions are miracles, and every word he says, an oracle.

Tartuffe, who knows his dupe and wants to use him, artfully dazzles him with a thousand false colors; his hypocrisy draws money out of Monsieur all the time, and assumes the right to find fault with every one of us. It's gone so far that even the stupid ass who acts as his servant takes a hand at lecturing us,

---

[4] Allusion to the *Fronde,* civil warfare from 1648 to 1653, mainly directed against Cardinal Mazarin and the queen mother, Anne of Austria, who were ruling during the minority of Louis XIV.

[5] *This is a servant speaking.* (Molière's note.)

and comes to sermonize us with ferocious looks, and throw out
our ribbons, our rouge, and our beauty spots. The other day,
the wretch tore up a handkerchief he found in a copy of the
Flower of the Saints, saying that we were committing a frightful crime by mixing holiness with the snares of the devil.

(*Re-enter* ELMIRE *and* DAMIS.)   (I. 3)

ELMIRE: You're lucky you weren't present for the harangue
she gave us at the door. But I saw my husband; since he didn't
see me, I shall go upstairs to wait for his arrival.[6]

CLÉANTE: I'll wait for him here to save time; I just want to
say good-day to him. (*Exit* ELMIRE.)

DAMIS: Mention my sister's wedding to him. I suspect that
Tartuffe is opposed to it and is forcing my father to these great
delays; you know, of course, why I'm interested in it. If like
passion kindles both my sister and Valère, the sister of that
friend, you know, is dear to me; and if we had to . . .

DORINE: He's coming. (*Exit* DAMIS.)

(*Enter* ORGON.)   (I. 4)

ORGON: Ah, my brother, good-day.

CLÉANTE: I was leaving, but I am very pleased to see you
back; the countryside is not much in flower just now.

ORGON: Dorine . . . (*To* CLÉANTE) My brother-in-law, wait
a moment, please. Would you allow me—to ease my mind—to
inquire a bit about the news here? (*To* DORINE) Has everything gone well these past two days? What have you been
doing? How is everyone?

DORINE: The day before yesterday, Madame had a fever all
day, with a headache that's frightful to imagine.

ORGON: And Tartuffe?

---

[6] Many have puzzled over the meaning of these words. Some have suggested that Orgon is cold toward his wife; others, that Elmire has a
warmer fire in her apartment, etc. The real reason may be that Molière
simply wanted her out of the way for the time being. This would be an
exception to Molière's technical excellence in motivating exits and entrances.

DORINE:

> Tartuffe? He's hale and hearty,
> Fat and sleek,
> Rosy lipped and pink of cheek.

ORGON: The poor fellow!

DORINE: In the evening she felt quite ill and her headache was still so painful that at supper she could touch nothing at all.

ORGON: And Tartuffe?

DORINE:

> He supped alone in front of her,
> And consumed with great devotion
> Two partridges and half a leg of mutton.

ORGON: The poor fellow!

DORINE: The whole night long she couldn't close her eyes because of a fever that kept her from sleeping, and we had to watch over her till daybreak.

ORGON: And Tartuffe?

DORINE:

> Urged on by a drowsiness quite agreeable,
> He went to his room upon rising from table;
> Then into his nice warm bed he leapt,
> Where, completely untroubled, till daylight he slept.

ORGON: The poor fellow!

DORINE: Finally, she let herself be persuaded to undergo a bloodletting, and relief followed immediately.

ORGON: And Tartuffe?

DORINE:

> He plucked up his courage as best he could,
> And, fortifying his soul against all ills,
> To make up for the blood that Madame had shed
> At breakfast he downed four swigs of the red.

ORGON: The poor fellow!

DORINE:

> They are *both* well at last;

And I shall go and inform Madame of your presence,
And the interest you take in her convalescence.

(*Exit.*) (I. 5)

CLÉANTE: She's laughing right in your face, brother, and, without meaning any offense, I must say that she's quite right. Has anyone ever heard of such a caprice? Can a man cast such a spell these days as to make you forget everything for him, so that after relieving his wretched condition in your house, you should come to the point of . . . ?

ORGON: Stop right there, my dear brother-in-law; you don't know the one you are speaking of.

CLÉANTE: All right, I don't know him, but after all, to know what kind of man he may be . . .

ORGON:

> My brother, he would enchant you, and your delights
>   would never end.
> He is a man . . . who . . . ah . . . a man . . . well, anyway,
>   a man.
> Who follows well his lessons enjoys a peace profound
> And looks upon the world as so much dung.
> Yes, I am becoming another man from my talks with
>   him;
> He teaches me to love nothing,
> From all affection he detaches my soul,
> And I could see my brother, children, mother, and wife
>   all die
> Without caring any more than that. (*He snaps his
>   fingers.*)

CLÉANTE: Such humane feelings, dear brother!

ORGON:

> Ah! if you had seen how I met him,
> You would have felt the same friendship for him.
> Each day he came to the church with an air so sweet
> And right across from me went down on his knees.
> He caught the eye of the whole congregation

By the warmth with which he uttered his prayer;
He sighed, he bent way down,
He moaned, and over and over he kissed the ground;
And when I left he ran ahead quickly
To offer me holy water in the entry.
His servant, who imitated him in every way,
Told me who he was and how poor he was,
And I would give him gifts; but, with his modesty,
He always wanted to give some back to me.
"It's too much," he would say. "It's twice too much.
I am not worthy that you should have pity on me."
And, when I refused to take it back,
He would pass it to the poor right in front of my eyes.
Finally, heaven chose for me to take him into my
    household,
And since that time everything in it seems to prosper.
He finds fault with everything, and even in my wife
I see him take—for the sake of my honor—an extreme
    interest;
He warns me about people who make eyes at her,
And he's six times more jealous of her than I am.
You wouldn't believe the extent of his zeal;
He counts the least little thing he does as a sin,
A trifle is enough to shock him,
To the point where he came the other day to denounce
    himself
For having caught a flea, while in prayer,
And killed it with excessive wrath.

CLÉANTE: Good heavens, Brother! I think you must be
crazy. Are you trying to make fun of me with your talk? And
what do you think that all this farcical . . .

ORGON: Brother, such talk smells of freethinking. Your soul
is slightly tainted with it, and I have preached to you a dozen
times that you will get yourself into bad trouble.

CLÉANTE: That's the way your kind always talk. They want
everyone to be blind as they are; to have a good pair of eyes

is being a freethinker, and anyone who doesn't worship empty
posturing has neither respect nor belief in holiness.

Come, come, all your speeches don't frighten me; I know
how I speak, and heaven sees my heart. We aren't all the
slaves of affectation; there is false piety just as there is false
bravery; and, just as on the field of honor the truly brave ones
make the least noise, the good and truly pious, in whose foot-
steps we should follow, are likewise those who posture least.

What! will you make no distinction between hypocrisy and
piety? You want to treat them on the same terms, and render
the same honor to the mask as to the face: to treat fraud and
sincerity as equals, confuse appearance with reality, esteem the
phantom as much as the person and the counterfeit as the
genuine?

Men, for the most part, are strangely made! They never find
natural rightness; the limits of reason are too small for them;
in each respect they go beyond its limits, and the noblest thing
they often spoil by trying to overdo it and exceed all measure.
This is just a passing remark, Brother.

ORGON: Yes, you are doubtless a revered scholar; all the
knowledge in the world has found its last refuge in you; you
alone are wise, you alone are enlightened, an oracle, a Cato in
our own times, and next to you all men are fools.

CLÉANTE: I am not, my brother, a revered scholar, and all
of knowledge has not taken refuge in me; but, in a word, the
sum total of my learning is that I *do* know how to distinguish
between the true and the false. And, just as I see no kind of
heroism more to be valued than perfect piety—nothing nobler
or more beautiful in the world than the holy fire of a true zeal
—likewise I consider nothing more odious than those out-and-
out charlatans, those pray-ers in the market place. With sacri-
legious and deceitful grimace, they misuse at their pleasure
everything that men hold most sacred and holy, and get off
scot-free with making sport of it. Having sold out their soul for
gain, those people make of their devotions both trade and
merchandise, and want to buy authority and honors with false

looks and affected transports. I'm talking about those people whom one sees take the road to heaven with uncommon fervor in order to speed to their fortune. With ardent prayers they go begging every day, and preach retreat from the world while *they* stay on in court.

They know how to fit their zeal to their vices; they're hasty, vindictive, faithless, full of tricks; and to destroy someone they insolently cloak their savage spite with the best interests of heaven. Their bitter wrath is all the more dangerous because they take up against us arms which people respect, so that people look on with approval when that passion sets out to assassinate us with a holy sword.

We see too many appear of that false nature, but the pious in heart are easy to recognize. Our own day, my dear brother, sets before our eyes some who can serve us as glorious examples. Look at Ariston, Polydore, Clitandre, look at Oronte, Alcidamas, Périandre—no one denies them that title. They aren't at all braggarts of virtue, you don't see in them that insufferable display, and their piety is human and gentle. They don't criticize all our actions—they feel there's too much arrogance in those corrections. And leaving the pride of words to others, it is by their actions that they reprove ours. The appearance of evil gets little support from them, and their soul is disposed to judge well of their neighbor. They have no cliques, no intrigues. The only business they mind is to lead a good life. They never go after a sinner tooth and nail; they attach their hatred to the sin alone, and don't try, with an excessive zeal, to outdo heaven in taking care of its own interests.

Those are my people, that's the way to act, there is the example we must set before us. To speak the truth, your man is not of that model. It's in all good faith that you glorify his zeal, but I think you are dazzled by a false luster.

ORGON: My dear sir, brother-in-law, are you quite finished?

CLÉANTE: Yes.

ORGON (*ironically*): I am your humble servant. (*He starts to leave.*)

CLÉANTE: Please, one word, Brother. Let's drop that subject. You know that Valère has your word to become your son-in-law.

ORGON: Yes.

CLÉANTE: You had set a date for that tender union.

ORGON: That is true.

CLÉANTE: Then why put off its celebration?

ORGON: I don't know.

CLÉANTE: Could you have some other thought in mind?

ORGON: Perhaps.

CLÉANTE: Would you want to go back on your word?

ORGON: I don't say that.

CLÉANTE: I think no obstacle can prevent you from keeping your promises.

ORGON: That's according. (*Shrugs.*)

CLÉANTE: Do you need so many subtleties to say one word? I have come to you at Valère's request.

ORGON: Heaven be praised!

CLÉANTE: But what shall I tell him?

ORGON: Anything you please.

CLÉANTE: But I have to know your plans. What are they?

ORGON: To do . . . what heaven wishes.

CLÉANTE: Come, come, let's speak straight out. Valère has your word. Will you keep it or not?

ORGON: Farewell. (*Exit.*)

CLÉANTE: I fear some misfortune for his love; I must warn him of all that goes on. (*Exit.*)

Act Two

(*Enter* ORGON. *He looks around and then opens a door leading offstage.*)

ORGON: Mariane.

MARIANE (*offstage*): Yes, Father.

ORGON: Come here. I want to speak with you in secret.

(*Enter* MARIANE.)

MARIANE: What are you looking for? (ORGON *looks in a small room on the right toward the front.*)

ORGON: I'm looking to see if there isn't someone there who might hear us, for that little place is just right for catching someone unawares. Now then, we're all set. Mariane, I have always recognized in you a quite docile spirit, and you have always been dear to me.

MARIANE: I am very grateful for my father's love.

ORGON: That's very well said, my dear, and to deserve it you must have no other care than to please me.

MARIANE: In doing so I take my greatest pride.

ORGON: Very good. What do you say about Tartuffe, our guest?

MARIANE: Who, me?

ORGON: You. Watch carefully how you answer.

MARIANE: Alas, I shall say whatever you please.

(DORINE *enters from behind and listens.*)

ORGON: That's the proper way to speak. Then tell me, my dear, that in his whole character great worth shines forth, that he has touched your heart, and that it would make you content if by my choice he were to become your husband. (MARIANE *suddenly shrinks backward in surprise.*) Eh?

32

MARIANE: Eh?

ORGON: What is it?

MARIANE: I beg your pardon?

ORGON: What?

MARIANE: Was I mistaken?

ORGON: What?

MARIANE: Who, Father, do you want me to say has touched my heart and would make me content if by your choice he were to become my husband?

ORGON: Tartuffe.

MARIANE: It's nothing of the kind, Father; I swear it. Why make me tell such a lie?

ORGON: But I want it to be the truth; and it's enough for you that I have decided it.

MARIANE: What! Father, you want . . .

ORGON: Yes, my dear, I intend to unite Tartuffe to my family by your marriage. He will be your husband, I have settled it; and since, concerning your wishes, I . . . (*Noticing* (II. 2) DORINE) What are you doing there? Curiosity must be pushing you pretty hard, dearie, to come and listen to us that way.

DORINE: Really, I don't know if the rumor was based on guesswork or chance, but I had heard talk about this marriage and I treated it as pure nonsense.

ORGON: What? Is it so unbelievable?

DORINE: So much so, sir, that I don't believe even you.

ORGON: I know the way to make you believe it.

DORINE: Yes, yes, you're telling us a funny story.

ORGON: I'm telling what you will shortly see.

DORINE: Nonsense!

ORGON (*to* MARIANE): My dear, what I am saying is quite serious.

DORINE: Come on, don't believe your father. He's joking.

ORGON: I tell you . . .

DORINE: No, no matter what, we won't believe you.

ORGON: Pretty soon my wrath . . .

DORINE: All right, we believe you, so much the worse for you. How, sir, can it be that with the look of a man of sense and that big beard in the middle of your face you would be crazy enough to want to . . .

ORGON: Listen, you have taken certain liberties in this household that don't please me at all; I'm telling you, dearie.

DORINE: Let's speak without growing angry, sir, I beg you. Are you trying to make fun of people with this plot? Your daughter is not the dish for a bigot—he has other affairs to think about; and besides, what does such a match bring you? With all your wealth, why go out and choose a son-in-law in rags . . . ?

ORGON:

> Be quiet. If he has nothing,
> Know that that's exactly why we should revere him.
> His wretched shape is certainly an honest wretchedness.
> It should exalt him far above mere worldly greatness,
> Since he really was deprived of his riches
> By his lack of care for the temporal
> And his powerful ties with the eternal.
> But my help will be able to give him the means to emerge
> From his difficulties and regain possession of his properties.
> They are fiefs that are renowned, with good reason, in his
> Province, and he, just as you see him, is of the real nobility.

DORINE:

> Yes, and he's the one who says so; that vanity,
> Sir, doesn't go well with piety,
> He who takes on the pure and holy life
> Should not exalt his name and birth so high,
> And the humble conduct of devotion

Does not fit well with outbursts of ambition.
Why all that pride? . . .
But you're offended by this discussion—
Let's forget his nobility and speak of his person.
Will you give in possession, without some pain,
A girl like her to a man like him?
Hadn't you better think of the properness
Of this marriage, and foresee its consequence?
Know that a girl's virtue is at stake
When in her marriage you frustrate her taste;
That the resolve to live as an honest woman
Depends on the kind of husband she's given,
And often those whom we point at in fun [1]
Themselves make their wives into what they become.
In short, it is hard to be faithful
To husbands built on a certain model;
Whoever gives to his daughter a man she hates
Will answer to heaven for the slips she makes.
Think to what perils your plan exposes you.

ORGON: I tell you I have to learn how to live from her!

DORINE: You couldn't do better than to follow my lessons.

ORGON: My dear, let's not waste time on these tales: I know what you need and I am your father. I had pledged you to Valère, but, besides the fact that they say he's inclined to gambling, I suspect him also of being something of a free-thinker—I haven't noticed him frequenting the churches.

DORINE: Do you want him to race there at exactly your hours, like those who go only to be seen?

ORGON:
I didn't ask your opinion about it.
Whatever, the other is on the best terms with heaven,
And that is a treasure second to none.
In all good things this marriage will exceed your desires;
It will be candied in sweetness and pleasures.
Together you'll live, in your faithful fervor,

[1] I.e., with the sign of the cuckold.

> Like two little children, like two turtledoves.
> To unhappy disputes you never will come,
> And you will make of him whatever you want.

DORINE: Her? She'll just make an ass [2] of him, I can assure you.

ORGON: Ay! What talk!

DORINE:

> I'm telling you, he's got the makings of one,
> And his inborn talent, sir, will carry the day,
> Over all the virtue your daughter will have.

ORGON: Stop interrupting me and see that you keep quiet, without putting your nose in where you have no business.

DORINE: I'm only speaking, sir, in your own best interests. (*She continually interrupts him at the moment when he turns around to speak to his daughter.*)

ORGON: You take too much trouble; please be quiet.

DORINE: If we didn't love you . . .

ORGON: I *don't want* to be loved.

DORINE: But, sir, I want to love you in spite of yourself.

ORGON: Oh-h-h!

DORINE: Your honor is dear to me, and I can't allow you to lay yourself open to everyone's mockery.

ORGON: Will you not be quiet?

DORINE: It's a matter of conscience to keep you from making such an alliance.

ORGON: Will you shut up, serpent, whose shameless barbs . . .

DORINE: Ah! You are religious and you lose your temper?

ORGON: Yes, I get in a rage at hearing all that twaddle, and I positively want you to shut up.

DORINE: All right. But even if I don't speak, I'll go on thinking just the same.

ORGON: Think if you want to, but make every effort not to

[2] I.e., a cuckold.

tell me about it, or . . . Enough. (*Turning back to his daughter.*) In my wisdom, I have weighed everything with mature deliberation.

DORINE (*supposedly to herself, but purposely loud enough for* ORGON *to hear*): I get furious at not being able to talk.

(*She becomes silent as soon as he turns his head.*)

ORGON: Without being a dandy, Tartuffe is made in such a way . . .

DORINE: Yes, a fine snout!

ORGON: That even if you should have no sympathy for all the other gifts . . .

(*He turns in front of her and looks at her with his arms crossed.*)

DORINE:
    Now she's well provided for!
    If I were in her place, a man certainly
    Would not force me in marriage with impunity,
    And I'd make him see, right after the wedding,
    That a woman always has one vengeance ready.

ORGON: So, no attention is going to be paid to what I say?

DORINE: What are you complaining about? I'm not talking to you.

ORGON: What are you doing then?

DORINE: I'm talking to myself.

ORGON: Very well. (*Aside*) To punish her extreme insolence, I'm going to have to give her the back of my hand. (*He gets in position to slap her face; and* DORINE, *every time he looks back at her, stands stiffly without speaking.*) . . . My dear, you must approve my plan. . . . Believe that the husband . . . I have chosen for you . . . (*To* DORINE) Why don't you talk to yourself?

DORINE: I have nothing to say to myself.

ORGON: Just one more little word.

DORINE: I don't feel like it.

ORGON (*aside*): Of course, I was watching for you.

DORINE: I'm not *that* stupid!

ORGON: In short, my dear, you must respond with obedience and show absolute deference to my choice.

DORINE (*running away*): I'd go to the devil before I'd take such a husband.

ORGON (*tries to slap her and misses*): My dear, that girl of yours is an absolute plague. I simply can't stay in the same house with her without sinning. I feel completely out of shape to continue. . . . Her impudent talk has set my mind on fire, and I'm going out for a walk to calm down a little. (*Exit.*)

(II. 3)   (*Re-enter* DORINE.)

DORINE: Tell me, have you lost your tongue, and do I have to play your part for you? Allow someone to propose such a mad project without the slightest word of resistance!

MARIANE: What do you want me to do against a father's absolute power? [3]

DORINE: Whatever's necessary to ward off such a threat.

MARIANE: What?

DORINE:

> Tell him the heart doesn't love through someone else;
> That you're not getting married for him but yourself;
> That since you're the one for whom the business is done,
> It's you—not him—whom the husband should please.
> And that if he finds his Tartuffe so delicious,
> He can marry him without any hindrance.

MARIANE: I admit a father has so much power over us that I have never had the strength to speak up for myself.

DORINE: Let's think this out. Valère has taken steps to marry you. Do you love him, please, or do you not?

[3] Under the monarchy parents had almost absolute power over their children.

MARIANE:

>Ah! How great is your injustice toward my love,
>Dorine! Need you ask me such a question?
>Have I not a hundred times disclosed to you my heart?
>And don't you know the full extent of my tender pas-
>sion?

DORINE: How do I know whether your mouth was speaking for your heart, or if this suitor has *really* stirred your affection?

MARIANE: You do me great wrong, Dorine, to doubt it—my true feelings have shone forth only too clearly.

DORINE: In short, you do love him?

MARIANE: Yes, with an extremity of passion.

DORINE: And, at least in appearance, he loves you the same?

MARIANE: I believe so.

DORINE: And likewise both of you are dying to be married to each other?

MARIANE: Certainly.

DORINE: What do you have in mind, then, about this other match?

MARIANE: To put myself to death if I am forced.

DORINE: Very good! That's a resource I hadn't thought of. To get out of trouble all you have to do is die. The cure is certainly wonderful. I get furious when I hear talk like that!

MARIANE: My goodness, Dorine, what a pet you're getting into! You don't sympathize with people in distress.

DORINE: I don't sympathize with people who talk twaddle and who, at the moment of decision, go limp, as you do.

MARIANE: But can I help it if I'm timid?

DORINE: But love demands firmness of heart.

MARIANE: But haven't I been firm in my love for Valère? And isn't it up to him to obtain my father's permission?

DORINE: But look, if your father is an absolute wild man, who is completely infatuated with his Tartuffe and calls off the match he had decided on, can you blame that on your sweetheart?

MARIANE: But, by a great refusal and signal scorn, shall I reveal a heart too smitten with its choice? Shall I put aside for him—however splendid his worth—womanly modesty and filial duty? And do you want my tender ardor displayed to all the world . . . ?

DORINE:

> No, no, I don't want a thing; I see you want to
> Belong to Monsieur Tartuffe, and now that I think of it
> I'd be wrong to turn you away from such an alliance.
> What reason would I have to combat your wishes?
> In itself it is quite a superior catch.
> Monsieur Tartuffe! Oh-ho! Is this just anybody being
>   proposed?
> Certainly, Monsieur Tartuffe, when properly consid-
>   ered,
> Is not a man—no, sir!—to be sneezed at,
> And it's no small fortune to be his better half.
> Already everyone crowns him with glory;
> He's a nobleman back home, a fine figure of a man.
> He has a ruddy ear and florid complexion;
> You'll live only too happily with such a husband.

MARIANE: My goodness . . .

DORINE: What joy you will have in your heart when you see yourself the wife of so handsome a husband!

MARIANE: Oh, please stop such talk and find me some way out of this marriage. I'm done for, I give in—I'm ready to do anything.

DORINE:

> No, a girl must obey her father,
> Even if he'd give her a monkey for a husband.
> Your lot is quite fine, why should you complain?
> You'll go by public coach to his little town,
> Which you'll find fruitful in uncles and cousins,

And you'll enjoy *so much* your conversations with them.
Right off you'll be taken out in high society;
For your welcome, you'll go to visit
Miladies the wives of the bailiff and the first assessor,
Who will honor you with a camp stool in some corner.[4]
There, at carnival time, you may hope for
A ball and the royal violins, namely two bagpipers,
And sometimes Punch and Judy and the organ-grinder.
However, if your husband . . .

MARIANE:
Ah, you're making me die!
Try to think of a plan to save my life.

DORINE (*ironically*): I am your humble servant.

MARIANE: Oh, Dorine, have pity.

DORINE: For your own punishment this thing will take place.

MARIANE: My dear girl!

DORINE: No!

MARIANE: If the avowals I have made . . .

DORINE: None of that. Tartuffe is your man, and you'll get a taste.

MARIANE:
You know that I have always confided only in you.
Please do . . .

DORINE: No, you have to be tartuffified.

MARIANE:
All right! Since you cannot be moved by my fate,
Leave me alone henceforth to my despair.
From desperation my heart will find its help,
And I know the infallible cure for all my ills.

(*She starts to leave.*)

4 In the seventeenth century, houses and even castles had very little furniture by present-day standards. The size of the chair (when one was offered) indicated the degree of honor the host or hostess wished to show the guest—here, just enough to be doubly insulting.

Dorine: Oh, there, there, now, come back, I'll stop being angry. A person has to have pity on you in spite of everything.

Mariane: You see, if I am exposed to this cruel martyrdom, I tell you, Dorine, I shall simply expire.

Dorine: Don't torment yourself—with a little skill we can prevent . . . But here is Valère, your sweetheart.

(II. 4)   (*Enter* Valère.)

Valère: Madame, people have begun to spread a piece of news which I did not know, and which is doubtless quite fine.

Mariane: What?

Valère: That you are marrying Tartuffe.

Mariane: It is true that my father has got this idea into his head.

Valère: Your father, madame . . .

Mariane: Has changed his plan. He has just finished proposing it to me.

Valère: What! Seriously?

Mariane: Yes, seriously; he has declared himself for this match in no uncertain tones.

Valère: And what action have you decided on, madame?

Mariane: I don't know.

Valère: That's an honest answer. You don't know?

Mariane: No.

Valère: No?

Mariane: What do you advise me?

Valère: *I* advise you to take this husband.

Mariane: You advise me to?

Valère: Yes.

Mariane: Really?

Valère: Certainly. The choice is illustrious and well worth listening to.

Mariane: All right, that is advice, sir, which I accept.

VALÈRE: You won't have much trouble in following it, I think.

MARIANE: No more than your heart suffered in giving it.

VALÈRE: *I* gave it to please *you,* madame.

MARIANE: And *I* shall follow it to please *you.*

DORINE (*aside*): Let's see what will come out of all this.

VALÈRE: Is that the way to love? And it was deceit when you . . .

MARIANE: Let's not speak of that, please. You told me straight out that I should accept for a husband the one they want to give me, and *I* declare that I intend to do so, since *you* give me that salutary advice.

VALÈRE: Don't excuse yourself with my intentions—you had already made up your mind, and are seizing upon a frivolous pretext to justify breaking your word.

MARIANE: It's true; that is well said.

VALÈRE: Of course, and your heart never had any real flame for me.

MARIANE: Alas! You may think so if you like.

VALÈRE: Yes, yes, if I like; but my offended heart will anticipate you, perhaps, in a similar plan, and I know where to take the offer of my hand.

MARIANE: Ah, I don't doubt it; and the passions that merit arouses . . .

VALÈRE: Heavens, let's leave merit out of it; I have very little, no doubt, and you are giving me the proof; but I have hope in the kindness another will have for me, and I know someone whose heart will give me refuge, and consent without pride to make up for my loss.

MARIANE: The loss is not great, and with this change you will console yourself quite easily . . .

VALÈRE:
    I shall do my best, and you may believe so.
    A heart that forgets us puts our honor at stake;
    To forget it, we too must apply all our care.

If one does not succeed, one must feign it at least;
And this weakness is never forgiven,
Of showing love when we are abandoned.

MARIANE: Doubtless this sentiment is noble and lofty.

VALÈRE: Quite right, and everyone ought to approve it. After all! Would you want me to keep forever in my soul the embers of my love for you, and see you pass, before my eyes, into another's arms, without taking elsewhere a heart which you will have none of?

MARIANE: On the contrary, that is what I hope for, and I wish it were already done.

VALÈRE: You wish it?

MARIANE: Yes.

VALÈRE: I have been insulted enough, madame; I shall straightway make you content. (*He takes a step to go away.*)

MARIANE: Very well.

VALÈRE (*returning*): Just remember that you're the one forcing my heart to this extreme effort. (*Departs.*)

MARIANE: Yes.

VALÈRE (*returning*): And that the plan I have conceived in my breast is merely following your example. (*Departs.*)

MARIANE: My example—so be it.

VALÈRE (*returning*): Enough; you will be punctually served. (*Departs.*)

MARIANE: That's fine.

VALÈRE (*returning*): You will never see me again as long as I live.

MARIANE: How delightful!

VALÈRE (*goes away, and, when he is near the door, turns around.*): Eh?

MARIANE: What?

VALÈRE: Didn't you call me?

MARIANE: I! You're dreaming.

VALÈRE: Well, then, I shall proceed on my way. Farewell, madame.

MARIANE: Farewell, monsieur.

DORINE: Well, *I* think you're losing your minds with this outlandish nonsense. I let you quarrel yourselves out just to see how far it would go. Hey, there! Monsieur Valère. (*She goes to stop him by the arm, and* VALÈRE *puts up a show of great resistance.*)

VALÈRE: Hey, what do you want, Dorine?

DORINE: Come here. (*Drags him into the room.*)

VALÈRE: No, no, resentment holds me in sway. Do not turn me aside from what *she* desired.

DORINE: Stop.

VALÈRE: No, you see, it's all settled.

DORINE: Ah!

MARIANE: He suffers at the sight of me, my presence drives him away—I shall do much better to leave him alone. (*Starts for the door opposite.*)

DORINE (*leaves* VALÈRE *and runs to* MARIANE): Now the other one! Where are you running off to?

MARIANE: Let me go.

DORINE: You must come back.

MARIANE: No, no, Dorine, it's useless to try to hold me back.

VALÈRE: It's clear that the sight of me tortures her, so it's probably better for me to free her from it. (*Going to the door.*)

DORINE (*leaves* MARIANE *and runs to* VALÈRE): Again? Devil take you if I'll allow it! Stop this playing around and come here, both of you. (*She pulls them together.*)

VALÈRE: But what is your plan?

MARIANE: What are you trying to do?

DORINE: Bring you back together and get you out of trouble. (*To* VALÈRE) Are you out of your head to make such a fuss?

VALÈRE: Didn't you hear how she talked to me?

DORINE (*to* MARIANE): Are *you* out of your head to have lost your temper?

MARIANE: Didn't you see the whole thing, how he treated me?

DORINE (*to* VALÈRE): Stupidity on both sides. She has no other thought but to keep herself for you—I am a witness. (*To* MARIANE) He loves only you, and has no other desire than to be your husband—I'll stake my life on it.

MARIANE: Then why give me such advice?

VALÈRE: Why ask it on such a subject?

DORINE: You're both out of your heads. Here, give me your hands, both of you. (*To* VALÈRE) Come on, you.

VALÈRE (*giving his hand to* DORINE): What good's my hand?

DORINE (*to* MARIANE): Oh, come on! Yours.

MARIANE (*also giving her hand to* DORINE): What good's all that?

DORINE: Good heavens! Quick, come forward. You both love each other more than you think.

VALÈRE (*to* MARIANE): Then don't be so distressed at doing things, and look at people a little without hatred. (MARIANE *turns her eye toward* VALÈRE *and gives a little smile.*)

DORINE: It's a simple fact, lovers are out of their minds!

VALÈRE: Look here, don't I have a right to complain about you? And, truthfully, aren't you mean to enjoy telling me something hurtful?

MARIANE: But you, aren't you the most ungrateful man . . .

DORINE: Let's leave this whole debate for another time, and think about avoiding this devilish marriage.

MARIANE: Tell us what means to make use of.

DORINE: We'll pull every string there is. This is all foolishness—your father is talking sheer nonsense. But, for your part, it's best to give the appearance of gentle consent to his folly, so that in case of emergency it will be easier to postpone this proposed marriage. By gaining time one finds a cure for everything. One time you'll put him off with some sudden sickness that requires a delay, another time you'll put him off with bad omens; you're upset because you passed a funeral on the street, broke a mirror, or dreamed of muddy water. Anyway, the main thing is that you cannot be united to anyone but him (*pointing to* Valère) unless you say yes. But, the better to win out, I think it's a good idea for you two not to be seen talking together. (*To* Valère) Go away right now and get your friends busy to make him keep his promise. We are going to stir up her brother's efforts and get the stepmother on our side. Farewell.

Valère (*to* Mariane): Whatever efforts we may all prepare, truly my greatest hope is in you.

Mariane (*to* Valère): I cannot answer for my father's will, but I will belong to none but Valère.

Valère: You overwhelm me with joy! And whoever may dare . . .

Dorine: Ah! Lovers are never tired of babbling. Go away, I tell you.

Valère (*takes a step and returns*): Anyway . . .

Dorine: What a chatterbox! (*Pushing each one by the shoulder.*) You go that way and you go the other.

Act Three

(DAMIS, DORINE)

DAMIS:

    May lightning strike me dead on the spot,

    May I be called the greatest of cads,

    If respect or power can make me stop,

    And if I don't strike some blow on my own.

DORINE:

    Please, calm your storm;

    Your father merely mentioned it;

    One does not carry out all one's ideas,

    And the way is long from the thought to the deed.

DAMIS: I've got to stop that ass's plot and give him a couple of words in the ear.

DORINE: Ah! gently! As for him and your father, leave it up to your stepmother. She has some influence with Tartuffe; he's agreeable to everything she says and might well have some sweet feeling for her. Would to heaven it were true! Wouldn't that be fine! Anyway, for your sake she has sent for him; she wants to sound him out on the marriage that bothers you, to find out his feelings and to let him know what an unpleasant mess might arise if he should encourage this plan. His valet said he is praying and I couldn't see him, but the valet said he was going to come down. So go away, please, and let me wait for him.

DAMIS: I can be present for the whole interview.

DORINE: Not at all; they must be alone.

DAMIS: I won't say a thing to him.

DORINE: You're joking—everyone knows about you and your temper—that's the real way to spoil things. Go away.

DAMIS: No, I want to see, without getting angry.

DORINE: What a pest you are! He's coming—go away. (DAMIS *hides in the little room, unnoticed by* DORINE.)

(*Enter* TARTUFFE *from the outer door, upstage.*)   (III. 2)

TARTUFFE (*perceiving* DORINE, *speaks to his servant, off stage*):

Laurent, hang up my hair shirt along with my lash,[1]
And at all times pray to heaven for guidance.
I'm going out; if I should have any visitors,
I have gone to share my poor alms with the prisoners.[2]

DORINE: What affectation and swaggering!

TARTUFFE: What do you wish?

DORINE: To tell you . . .

TARTUFFE (*takes out a handkerchief*): Ah! good heavens, please! Before speaking take this handkerchief.

DORINE: What?

TARTUFFE:

Cover that breast which I must not see.
By sights such as those, souls are wounded,
And it makes guilty thoughts come into one's head.

DORINE:

Are you, then, an easy mark for temptation?
Does the flesh on your senses make such an impression?
I'm sure I don't know how *your* fever goes up,
But *I* am not so quick and ready to lust;
I could see you naked from head to foot,
And your whole skin wouldn't tempt me a bit.

TARTUFFE:

Put a little modesty in your speech,
Or this very minute I shall leave.

DORINE: No, no, it is I who shall leave you in peace; I have

---

[1] Instruments used to punish oneself ("mortification of the flesh") in extreme forms of penance.

[2] Visiting prisoners was a work of mercy recommended to the faithful by the Council of Trent.

only one thing to tell you. Madame is coming down to this
parlor and asks the favor of a word with you.

TARTUFFE: Alas! with pleasure.

DORINE (*to herself*): Look at him soften up! I'll certainly
stick to what I said before.

TARTUFFE: Is she coming soon?

DORINE: I think I hear her. Yes, it's she. I'll leave you together. (*Exit.*)

(III. 3)   (*Enter* ELMIRE.)

TARTUFFE:
>   May you be given by the infinite goodness of heaven
>   Health in both body and soul forever,
>   And may your days be blessed as much as desires
>   The humblest of those whom its love inspires.

ELMIRE: I am much obliged for this pious wish. But let us
sit down and be more comfortable.

TARTUFFE: Do you feel recovered from your illness?

ELMIRE: Quite well—the fever soon lost hold.

TARTUFFE:
>   My prayers are not worthy enough
>   To have drawn down this grace from above,
>   But I have made to heaven no pious instance
>   For causes other than your convalescence.

ELMIRE: Your zeal went to too much trouble for me.

TARTUFFE: One cannot cherish too much your dearest
health, and to bring it back I would have given my own.

ELMIRE: That's pushing Christian charity pretty far—I am
much indebted for all your kindness.

TARTUFFE: I do much less than you deserve.

ELMIRE: I wanted to speak to you about something in secret
—I'm very glad no one is listening.

TARTUFFE: I, too, am delighted, and it is certainly sweet for
me, madame, to find myself alone with you. It is an oppor-

tunity that I have begged of heaven, without its being granted until this moment.

ELMIRE: For my part, I desire a moment's chat in which you open your whole heart, hiding nothing.

TARTUFFE:

> And, as a unique blessing, my only desire
> Is to bare my soul before your eyes,
> And swear to you that the rows I have raised
> About the visitors whom your beauty fascinates
> Are not the result of hatred for you,
> But rather a flight of zeal by which I am moved,
> And a pure transport . . .

ELMIRE: I don't take it amiss; I feel that you take this care for my salvation's sake.

TARTUFFE (*he squeezes the tips of her fingers*): Yes, madame, of course; and my fervor is such . . .

ELMIRE: O-oh! You're squeezing too hard.

TARTUFFE: From excessive zeal. To do you harm was never my intention, and I would far rather . . . (*He puts his hand on her knee.*)

ELMIRE: What is your hand doing there?

TARTUFFE: I'm feeling your dress; the material is silken.

ELMIRE: Oh! please stop; I'm very ticklish. (*She pushes her chair back, and* TARTUFFE *brings his nearer.*)

TARTUFFE: My goodness! The workmanship of this lace (*around her neck and bosom*) is marvelous. The work they do these days seems a miracle; never have things been done so well in every way.

ELMIRE: That's true. But let's get down to our business for a moment. I have heard that my husband wants to take back his word and give his daughter to you; tell me, is that true?

TARTUFFE:

> To tell the truth—though he has mentioned something
>   like—

Madame, *that* is not the happiness for which I sigh,
And elsewhere I see the marvelous grace
Of the bliss that is my only aspiration.

ELMIRE: That's because you can love nothing here below.

TARTUFFE: My breast does not enclose a heart of stone.

ELMIRE: Oh, *I* am sure that all your sighs are directed
towards heaven, and that nothing earthly stays your desires.

TARTUFFE:
The love that binds us to beauty eternal
Does not quench in us all love for the temporal.
And our senses may easily be charmed
By the perfect works that heaven has formed.
Its loveliness reflected shines in those of your nature,
But in you it displays its rarest treasures.
On your face is painted its loveliest beauty,
To take eyes unawares and ravish the heart away.
I could not look on you, O perfect creature,
Without admiring in you the Author of nature.
And with fervent love I felt my heart stricken
By the fairest portrait in which He is depicted.
At first I feared that this secret ardor
Was an ambush of the Prince of Darkness,
And my heart resolved to flee from your sight,
Believing you a hindrance on the way to paradise.
But at last I knew, O adorable beauty,
That this passion can be unguilty—
That I can reconcile it with modest behavior,
And that is why I let my heart surrender.
It is, I confess, an act of great boldness,
This offering of love, to you addressed;
But I expect, in my vows, all from your mercy,
Presuming naught from my infirmity.
In you is my hope, my weal, my rest;
On you depends my torment or my blessedness;
And I shall be at last, by your sole decree,
Blessed, if you will it, cursed, if you please.

ELMIRE: The declaration is quite gallant, but, to tell the truth, it's somewhat surprising. It seems to me you should have steeled your heart a little more and thought more reasonably about such a notion. Pious as you are, whom everyone calls . . .

TARTUFFE:

> Ah! Though I am pious, I am none the less a man;
> And when one sees your divine attractions,
> One's heart lets go and doesn't reason.
> I know that such talk from me seems strange;
> But, madame, after all, I am not an angel,
> And, if you condemn this confession I make,
> The blame must be placed on your own fascinations.
> As soon as I saw their superhuman splendor
> You became queen of my spiritual nature.
> Your unspeakably sweet, divine regard
> Broke down the resistance of my obdurate heart;
> Fasting, tears, prayers—all—it swept aside,
> And toward your charms all my vows inclined.
> My looks and sighs have told you this a thousand times,
> And now, to tell it more clearly, my tongue I employ.
> If your soul looks down with any compassion
> On your unworthy slave and his tribulations,
> If your mercy should vouchsafe to give me solace
> And stoop as low as my utter insignificance,
> For you I shall have, O vessel of fragrance,
> Forever a matchless allegiance.
> Your reputation runs no risk with me,
> Where I'm concerned has no ill luck to fear.
> All the courtly fops that women are mad for
> Are noisy in their deeds and vain in their words;
> Constantly their progress they boast,
> Receiving no favor they do not disclose;
> Their indiscreet tongues, in which women confide,
> Besmirch the altar of their heart's sacrifice.
> But people like us burn with a flame that is quiet,
> With us one is always assured of one's secret.

> The care which we take of our reputation
> Is a firm guarantee to the person beloved,
> And in us can be found, by accepting our heart,
> Love without scandal and pleasure without fear.

ELMIRE: I have been listening to your rhetoric, and you have made me a declaration in rather strong terms. Aren't you afraid I might feel like telling my husband about this amorous fervor, and that the sudden news of such a love might very well alter his friendship for you?

TARTUFFE:

> I know that you have too much clemency,
> And that you will pardon my temerity;
> That you will forgive me the human weakness,
> The violent raptures, of a love that offends;
> And that you will consider, as you look at yourself,
> That one cannot be blind, and a man is but flesh.

ELMIRE: Perhaps others would react differently, but I wish to show my discretion. I shall not repeat this to my husband, but in return I want something from you: that is, that you urge straight out, and with no double-dealing, the union of Valère with Mariane; that you yourself renounce this unjust use of power which would enrich you at another's expense, and . . .

(III. 4)   DAMIS (*coming out of the room in which he had hidden*): No, madame, no, this news must be spread far and wide. I was in this place where I could hear everything; the kindness of heaven seems to have led me there to confound the pride of a traitor who's doing me harm, to open a path of vengeance on his hypocrisy and insolence, to undeceive my father and show him in broad daylight the soul of a scoundrel who speaks to you of love.

ELMIRE: No, Damis, it's enough if he behaves himself and tries to deserve the forgiveness I pledge. Since I have promised, don't break my word. It's not my nature to create a row; a woman laughs at that kind of nonsense and never troubles her husband's ears with it.

DAMIS: You have your reasons for behaving that way, and I have mine for acting otherwise. It would seem mockery to spare him; the impudent pride of his bigotry has triumphed only too much over my righteous anger and fomented only too much disorder in our household. The swindler has governed my father too long and done an ill turn to my passion and Valère's too. Father must have his eyes opened to this traitor, and heaven has offered me an easy way to do it. I am grateful for this chance—it is too good to neglect; I would deserve that heaven snatch it back from me if I had it in my hands and didn't use it.

ELMIRE: Damis . . .

DAMIS: No, if you please, I must have it my own way. My heart is bursting with joy, and it's all useless talk to try to make me give up the pleasure of vengeance. Without going any further, I'm going to settle this thing, and here is just what I need.

(Enter ORGON.*)*   **(III. 5)**

We are going to treat your arrival, Father, to a piece of fresh news that will greatly surprise you. You are well paid back for all your pampering, and Monsieur makes you a nice return on your fondness. His great zeal for you has just declared itself. It falls nothing short of dishonoring you; I caught him here making the outrageous confession to Madame of a guilty passion. She has a sweet nature and too discreet a heart —she was determined to keep it quiet, but I can't indulge such shamelessness. I think that keeping it from you is doing you offense.

ELMIRE: Yes, I maintain that we should never disturb a husband's peace of mind with that kind of idle talk; honor cannot depend on such trifles, and it's enough for us to know how to defend ourselves. Those are my feelings, and you would have said nothing, Damis, if I had had any influence on you. *(Exit.)*

(III. 6)   ORGON: What do I hear, O Lord, can it be true?

TARTUFFE:

>   Yes, dear brother, I am a wicked, guilty,
>   Wretched sinner, full of all iniquities,
>   The greatest scoundrel who ever lived.
>   My life is soiled and stained at every minute;
>   It's nothing but a mass of crimes and filth,
>   And I see that heaven, to chastise me,
>   Is seeking now to mortify me.
>   However gross a crime may be alleged,
>   I refrain from the pride of self-defense.
>   Believe what you are told, arm your wrath,
>   And drive me, like a criminal, from your home;
>   The measure of my shame could not fail
>   To be much less than I deserve.

ORGON (*to his son*): Ah, traitor! do you dare, with this falsehood, try to tarnish the pureness of his virtue?

DAMIS: What! The sham meekness of that hypocrite soul will make you impugn . . .

ORGON: Shut up, you cursed plague!

TARTUFFE: Ah! let him speak; you accuse him wrongly, and you would do much better to believe his account.[3] Why should you favor me so much in such a matter? After all, do you know what I am capable of? Do you trust, dear brother, in my looks? And just because of what you see, do you think I really am any better? No, no, you are letting appearances deceive you, and I am nothing less—alas!—than what they think. Everyone takes me for a good man, but the pure truth is that I have no worth. (*Speaking to* DAMIS) Yes, my dear son, speak, call me traitor, vile, debauched, thief, murderer; heap on me names more hateful still; I don't deny it—I have deserved them, and I will suffer the shame on my knees (*he kneels*) as a disgrace earned by the crimes of my life.

---

[3] Tartuffe uses even the truth to deceive "when he can be certain that it will be taken for the opposite. . . . These statements are true, but they are the reverse of sincere. They overturn the universal assumptions of language . . ." (W. G. Moore, *Molière: A New Criticism*, p. 64).

ORGON (*to* TARTUFFE): Dear brother, this is too much. (*To his son*) Doesn't your heart surrender, traitor?

DAMIS: What! His talk can lead you so far astray as . . .

ORGON: Shut up, villain! (*To* TARTUFFE) Dear brother, oh! get up, please! (TARTUFFE *rises.*) (*To his son*) Vile . . . !

DAMIS: He can . . .

ORGON: Shut up.

DAMIS: This infuriates me! What! I pass . . .

ORGON: If you say a single word, I'll break both your arms.

TARTUFFE: Dear brother, in the name of heaven, don't get angry. I would suffer the severest torture rather than have him receive the slightest scratch for my sake.

ORGON (*to his son*): Ungrateful . . . !

TARTUFFE: Leave him in peace. If I must intercede for him on both knees . . . (*He kneels.*)

ORGON (*overcome by emotion also kneels, embraces* TARTUFFE *and tries to get him to rise*): Alas! You don't mean it? (*He arises rapidly;* TARTUFFE, *more leisurely.*) (*To his son*) Wretch, behold his goodness.

DAMIS: So . . .

ORGON: Peace!

DAMIS: What, I . . .

ORGON: Peace, I tell you! I'm well aware of the motive that makes you attack him. You all hate him, and today I see wife, children, and valets in a rage against him. Shamelessly you put everything to work to get this pious person out of my house, but the more efforts you make to banish him, the more I will use to keep him, and I shall hasten to give him my daughter, to confound the pride of my whole family.

DAMIS: You plan to make her accept his hand?

ORGON: Yes, traitor, this very evening, to drive you all into a fury. Ah! I will stand up to all of you and make you realize that I *will* be obeyed and that I am the master. Come on, take it back this instant, rascal; throw yourself at his feet and ask for pardon.

Damis: Who, me? From this wretch, who by his imposture . . .

Orgon: Ah! you resist, beggar, and insult him? A stick, a
stick! (*To* Tartuffe) Don't hold me back. (Tartuffe *has
made no move to do so.*) (*To his son*) Come on! Leave my
house at once and never dare to come back again.

Damis: Yes, I shall leave, but . . .

(III. 7) Orgon: Quick, get out. (*Exit* Damis. Orgon *goes to the door
and shouts after him.*) Villain, I cut you off from your inheritance and give you my curse besides. (Orgon *returns.*) Offend a
saintly person like that!

Tartuffe: O heaven! Forgive him the pain he does unto
me. (*To* Orgon) If you only knew how unhappy it makes
me to see them try to degrade me in the eyes of my dear
brother . . .

Orgon: Alas!

Tartuffe: Just the thought of that ingratitude makes my
soul suffer such harsh torment . . . The horror it makes me
feel . . . My heart is so heavy I cannot talk, and I shall probably die.

Orgon (*runs all in tears to the door through which he has
chased his son*): Wretch! I repent that my hand spared you,
and didn't strike you dead on the spot. Calm yourself, dear
brother, and don't be sad.

Tartuffe:

> Let us break, let us break off this painful discussion.
> I look about me and see that I bring great dissension,
> And I feel I must leave here, dear brother.

Orgon: What! You don't mean it?

Tartuffe: I am despised, and I see they are trying to make
you suspect my good faith.

Orgon: What is the difference! Do you see my heart listen
to them?

Tartuffe: They cannot fail to pursue it, and these same

accounts which you now reject . . . Perhaps another time you will listen.

ORGON: No, dear brother, never.

TARTUFFE: Ah, dear brother, a wife can easily mislead a husband's soul.

ORGON: No, no.

TARTUFFE: By going far away from here, let me quickly remove all their grounds for attacking me so.

ORGON: No, you will stay; it's a matter of life and death to me.

TARTUFFE: All right then, I shall have to mortify myself. However, if you would . . .

ORGON: Ah!

TARTUFFE: So be it, let's speak of it no more. But I know how one must behave in such matters. Honor is a delicate thing, and friendship obliges me to forestall rumors and grounds for suspicion; I shall flee your wife and you won't see me . . .

ORGON: No, in spite of them all, you will keep her company. To drive people to fury is my greatest joy, and I want you to be seen with her constantly. That's still not all; to defy them all even better, I want no other heir but you, and I will go immediately and make over to you, in proper form, a gift of all my fortune. A good and true friend whom I take as my son-in-law is far dearer to me than son, wife, or kin. Won't you accept my proposal?

TARTUFFE: May heaven's will be done in all things.

ORGON (*aside*): The poor fellow! (*To* TARTUFFE) Let's go quickly and draw it up in writing, and may the envious die of spite! (*Exeunt.*)

Act Four

(*Enter* CLÉANTE *and* TARTUFFE.)

CLÉANTE: Yes, everybody's talking about it, and—you may take my word—the scandal is not to your credit. I'm glad I ran across you, sir, so I can tell you my thoughts straight out in a couple of words. I shan't delve into the details; I shall pass over that and accept things at their worst. Let us suppose that Damis acted improperly and accused you wrongly; is it not up to a Christian to pardon the offense and smother in his heart all desire for vengeance? And should you allow a son to be banished from his father's house because of your dispute? I tell you again —and I'm speaking frankly—there's no one, high or low, who isn't scandalized by the situation. If you take my advice, you will smooth everything over and not push things to their bitter end. Sacrifice your wrath to God, and bring the son back into his father's good graces.

TARTUFFE: Alas, I would be glad to, for myself; I harbor no bitterness against him, sir. I forgive him all—I blame him for nothing, and would like to serve him with the greatest good will; but it would be incompatible with the best interests of heaven, and if he comes back here, it will be up to me to leave. After his action—the like of which has never been seen —any relations between us would cause a scandal. Goodness knows what people would think of it; they'd impute it to sheer politics on my part, and everyone would say that, knowing myself guilty, I was feigning a charitable zeal for my accuser, that I fear him in my heart and want to handle him with care and pledge him secretly to silence.

CLÉANTE: You are paying us now with counterfeit excuses, and all your reasons, sir, are too tenuous. Why do you take on the interests of heaven? Does it need us to punish the guilty? Leave heaven to avenge itself, and think only of the forgiveness it prescribes for offenses. Pay no attention to human judgments when you follow the sovereign commands of heaven. What! The insipid care for people's opinion will prevent you from doing a good and praiseworthy deed? No, no, let us always do what heaven prescribes, and trouble our minds with no other care.

TARTUFFE: I have already told you that I forgive him in my heart, and that, sir, is doing what heaven ordains; but after today's scandal and insult, heaven does not ordain that I live with him.

CLÉANTE: And does it ordain, sir, that you open your ears to his father's impulsive fancy and accept the gift of property to which you have no rightful claim?

TARTUFFE: Those who know me will not think it a result of self-interest in my soul. All the goods of this world have little appeal for me; I am not dazzled by their deceitful splendor, and if I have decided to receive this gift that the father has chosen to make, it is—to tell the truth—solely because I fear that great fortune might fall into wicked hands, that it might find its way, by inheritance, to people who would put it to criminal use in the world, and not employ it, as I plan to, for the glory of heaven and the good of their neighbor.

CLÉANTE: Ah, monsieur, do not hold such exquisite fears, which could cause the complaints of a rightful heir. Don't trouble yourself about a thing, and just let him possess his fortune at his own risk. And remember that it is much better for him to misuse it than for you to be accused of defrauding him.

I am simply amazed that you could submit to the proposal without embarrassment; for, after all, does true religion have some maxim that teaches us to despoil the legitimate heir? And if it is true that heaven has placed some insuperable barrier in the way of your living with Damis, wouldn't it be better for you, as a gentleman, to make a prudent exit than to allow— against all reason—a son to be driven out of his house on your account? Believe me, on the score of your *decency*, sir . . .

Tartuffe: It is, sir, three-thirty; certain religious duties call me *(points to his room)*, and you will forgive me for leaving you so soon. *(Exit.)*

Cléante: Ah!

(Enter Elmire, Mariane, Dorine.*)*

Dorine: Please, sir, help us on her behalf; her soul is in mortal pain; at every moment she falls into despair when she thinks of the betrothal her father has set for this evening. He's on his way here; let's unite our efforts, please, and try, by force or by wit, to unhinge this wretched plan that has us all upset.

(Enter Orgon, *with a legal document.)*

Orgon: Ah! I'm delighted to find you all gathered together. *(To* Mariane*)* I have here in this contract something to make you laugh, and you know already what that means.

Mariane *(on her knees)*:
    Dear father, in the name of heaven, which knows my
       grief,
    By all that to your heart may plead,
    Of your paternal rights so much release
    That from such obedience my love may be freed.
    Do not compel me, by harsh rule,
    To complain to heaven of what I owe you;
    And this life, dear father, of which you were the maker—
    Do not, alas, make it utterly hateful.
    If you forbid me my sweetest hope,
    To belong to the one I make bold to love,
    At least, by your mercy, which at your knees I implore,
    Spare me the grasp of one whom I loathe,
    And do not push me to some act of despair
    By using on me all of your power.

Orgon *(aside, feeling himself softening)*: Come, come, steady, my heart; no human weakness!

Mariane:
    Your favors to him do not distress me;

Make them shine forth. Give him your fortune,
And, if that isn't enough, give him mine too.[1]
I consent cheerfully and give it up forever.
But at least don't carry this as far as my person;
And permit me, amidst a convent's austerities,
To wear out the sad days that heaven has allotted me.

ORGON: Ah! So there's one of those who become nuns as soon as a father combats their sweet passion! Stand up! The more your heart shrinks from accepting him, the more meritorious is the act. Mortify your senses with this marriage, and don't give me any more chatter.

DORINE: What! . . .

ORGON: Shut up, you. Mind your own business; I forbid you straight out to dare say a single word.

CLÉANTE: If you would allow a word of advice in answer to . . .

ORGON: My dear brother, your advice is the best in the world; it is very logical, and I value it highly, but you will permit me not to take it.

ELMIRE *(to her husband)*: I am dumbfounded at what I see—your blindness amazes me. He must really have turned your head to make you so prejudiced that you don't believe us about what happened today.

ORGON: I am your humble servant, and I believe in the appearance. I know how sympathetic you are to my rascally son—you were afraid to give the lie to the trick he tried to play on that poor fellow. Anyway, you were too calm to be believed; you would have appeared much more upset.

ELMIRE: Must our honor fly up in arms at a simple declaration of amorous fancy? Can we answer it only with flaming eyes and abusive tongue? For my part I don't like any uproar about it—I simply laugh at such remarks. I like women to be modest without harshness; I don't agee at all with those savage prudes whose honor is armed with claws and teeth, who want to com-

---

[1] Inherited from her mother's estate. Elmire is Orgon's second wife.

mit mayhem on people at the slightest word. May heaven preserve me from such goodness! I want a virtue that isn't shrewish; and I think that a cool and discreet refusal is no less powerful in chilling passion.

ORGON: Well, I know the whole business, and I'm not thrown off the track.

ELMIRE: I'm still amazed at this bizarre weakness. But what would happen to your disbelief if I made you see that we're telling you the truth?

ORGON: See?

ELMIRE: Yes.

ORGON: Nonsense!

ELMIRE: What! Suppose I found a way to make you see it clear as day?

ORGON: Idle tales!

ELMIRE: What a man! At least give me an answer. I'm not asking you to have faith in us; but now let's suppose that from a certain well-chosen spot we made you see and hear everything clearly, then what would you say about your fine gentleman?

ORGON: In that case I would say . . . I wouldn't say anything, because it can't be.

Elmire: The error has endured too long, and my lips have been charged too much with imposture. I must have the pleasure right now of making you a witness to everything you've been told.

ORGON: Agreed—I'll take you up on that. We shall see your skill and how you can carry out that promise.

ELMIRE (*to* DORINE): Send him to me.

DORINE: His wits are sharp—it may not be so easy to trap him.

ELMIRE: No, one is easily duped by what one loves, and vanity undertakes to deceive itself. Send him down to me. (*Speaking to* CLÉANTE *and* MARIANE) You, withdraw. (*Exeunt.*)

(IV. 4) (*To* ORGON) Let's pull up this table. . . . Get under it.

ORGON: What!

ELMIRE: You must be well hidden.

ORGON: Why under this table?

ELMIRE: Oh, heavens! Let me manage; I have my plan in mind and you will judge it. Get under there, I say, and when you're there don't let yourself be seen or heard.

ORGON: I must admit my indulgence is going pretty far, but I have to see how you'll get out of this business you've taken on.

ELMIRE: I don't think you'll have any comeback. (*To her husband, who is under the table*) Remember, I'm going to bring up a strange topic. Don't be at all scandalized. Whatever I may say must be allowed me, since it's to convince you, as I promised. Since I am reduced to this, I am going to use sweetness; to make that hypocrite soul lay aside his mask, I shall encourage his shameless desires and leave a clear field to his temerity. Since I'm going to play at being responsive to him for you alone—just to trip him up—I'll be ready to stop as soon as you give in, and things will go only so far as you desire. It's up to you to put a stop to his mad passion, when you think things have been carried far enough. It's up to you to spare your wife and expose me to no more than is necessary to open your eyes. These are your interests, you know—you will be the master, and . . . someone's coming; be still and don't show yourself.

(*Enter* TARTUFFE.)   (IV. 5)

TARTUFFE: I was told that you wished to speak to me in here.

ELMIRE: Yes, there are secrets to be revealed to you. But pull that door shut first and look around everywhere for fear of being caught; an encounter like the one a little while ago is certainly not what we need right now. I've never been so startled in my life; Damis gave me quite a fright on your account, and you must have seen how I did all I could to break off his plan and calm his fits of temper. However, I was so up-

set that it didn't occur to me to contradict him; but, thank
heavens, everything turned out for the best, and, as a result,
things are more secure than ever. You are held in such esteem
that the storm just vanished—my husband is unable to suspect
you. He wants to fly in the teeth of scandal by keeping us together all the time; that is why we can be closeted here with
no fear of blame, and that is what permits me to reveal a heart
perhaps a bit too prompt in suffering your passion.

TARTUFFE: This language is rather difficult to understand,
madame; awhile ago you spoke in a different style.

ELMIRE:

Ah! If you are angry over such a refusal,
How little a woman's heart is known to you!
And how little you know what it wants to express
When it struggles so weakly in self-defense.
Our modesty always opposes, at such a moment,
Any proffer of tender sentiment.
However fit we think the love that wins,
We find it somewhat shameful to admit.
At first we put up some resistance, but in our manner
We make it clear that our heart surrenders,
That our lips oppose our wishes for the sake of honor,
And that such refusals promise everything.
Of course, this is a rather frank admission,
And modesty would call for more restraint;
But, since the word has now escaped me,
Would I have tried so hard to stop Damis?
Would I, please, have listened quite so sweetly,
And heard to the end the offer of your heart?
Would I have taken it the way I did,
If the offer of that heart weren't somehow pleasing?
And when I tried, myself, to make you turn down
The wedding plans that had just been announced,
What should that request have made you understand,
If not the care for you that we have taken on,
And the pain that would ensue if the union proposed
Should share a heart we'd rather keep alone?

TARTUFFE:

    To be sure, madame, it is sweetness extreme
    From lips one loves to hear words such as these;
    Their honey flows through all my senses,
    Pouring forth a novel fragrance.
    The joy of pleasing you is my supreme endeavor;
    In your desires my heart finds blessedness.
    But this heart now asks the liberty
    To question its felicity.
    I might think those words an honest stratagem
    To make me reject an approaching marriage;
    And, if I may speak plainly with you,
    I will not trust such sweet discourse,
    Until some sample of your favors, which I sigh for,
    Bestowed on me, confirms what has been stated,
    And implants in my soul a steadfast faith
    In the enchanting kindness you show for me.

ELMIRE (*coughs to warn her husband*):

    What! You want to move with such haste
    And drain a heart of its sweetness straightway?
    A person kills herself making the tenderest declaration,
    But that's still not enough for you;
    Can't you be satisfied until things
    Are pushed to the ultimate favors?

TARTUFFE:

    The more unworthy of blessing, the less one dares to
      hope.
    Our wishes aren't confirmed by talk alone.
    One easily doubts such glorious fate,
    And one wants to possess it before one believes it.
    And I—who feel unworthy of your goodness—
    I distrust the fortune of my boldness;
    I believe in nothing until you, madame,
    By something real, convince my passion.

ELMIRE:

    Heavens! your love is acting like a tyrant,

And stirs up strange disorder in my mind!
Our hearts are taken in such fierce command,
And with what violence it wants what it desires!
What! Is there no way to ward off pursuit—
Don't you give one time to breathe?
Is it right of you to be so adamant,
To give no quarter in the things you demand,
And by your urgent efforts take advantage
Of the weakness people have for you?

TARTUFFE:

But if with compassionate eye you view my worship,
Then why refuse me certain proof?

ELMIRE:

But how can one consent to what you want
Without offending heaven, of which you always talk?

TARTUFFE:

If heaven is all that's opposed to my wishes,
To remove such a hindrance means nothing to me,
And that should not restrain your heart.

ELMIRE:

But they frighten us so with heaven's decrees.

TARTUFFE:

I can dispel for you such silly fears,
Madame—I know the art of removing scruples.
Heaven forbids—it's true—certain satisfactions; [2]
But one can arrange a give-and-take settlement.
According to differing needs, there is a science
Of stretching the fetters of our conscience,
And rectifying the evil of the action
With the purity of our intention.[3]
Concerning those secrets, madame, I can instruct you—
You have only to let yourself be guided.

[2] *This is a scoundrel speaking.* (Molière's note.)
[3] Direction of intention, one of the subdivisions of casuistry. See Introduction, pp. ix–x.

Satisfy my desire and have no fear;
I'll take the entire responsibility on myself.

(ELMIRE *coughs again, loudly.*)

You are coughing hard, madame.

ELMIRE: Yes, I'm in terrible pain.

TARTUFFE: Would you like one of these licorice drops?

ELMIRE:
It must be an obstinate cold; I can see that
All the drops in the world won't help now.

TARTUFFE: This is certainly trying.

ELMIRE: Yes, more than one can say.

TARTUFFE:
Well, your scruple is easy to destroy;
You are assured of secrecy here;
Evil lies only in the stir created.
Public scandal is what makes the offense,
And it's not sinning to sin in silence.

ELMIRE (*after having coughed some more*):
Well, I see I shall have to agree to yield,
That I must consent to grant you all.
With anything short of that I cannot expect
You to be satisfied or willing to give in.
Of course it's unfortunate to come to this,
And it's in spite of myself that I cross this line;
But since you stubbornly reduce me to it,
Since you don't believe what you are told,
And have to have convincing proof,
I must make up my mind to it and give you satisfaction.
If this consent bears offense in itself,
Too bad for the one who forces me to violent means—
The fault surely can't be mine.

TARTUFFE: Yes, madame, I take all this on my shoulders,
and the thing in itself . . .

ELMIRE: Open the door, please, and see if my husband is not in that hallway.

TARTUFFE: Why do you need to worry about him? Between you and me, he is a man to lead about by the nose. He takes pride in all our tête-à-têtes, and I have brought him to the point where he could see everything and not believe it.

ELMIRE: Never mind. Please go out a minute and look carefully everywhere.

(IV. 6)   (*Exit* TARTUFFE.)

ORGON (*coming out from under the table*): There, I admit, is an abominable man! I can't get over it; this stuns me.

ELMIRE: What! Coming out so soon? You're joking. Go back under the cloth; it isn't time yet. Wait until the end to see positive proof, and don't trust in pure conjecture.

ORGON: No, nothing more wicked has come out of hell.

ELMIRE: My heavens, you mustn't jump to conclusions; let yourself be fully convinced before you give in, and don't do it hastily, for fear of being mistaken. (*She puts her husband behind her.*)

(IV. 7)   TARTUFFE (*entering*): Madame, all things conspire for my satisfaction; I have looked through this whole suite—no one is here, and my soul, delighted . . . (*He advances toward* EL-MIRE *with open arms. She steps aside, revealing* ORGON.)

ORGON: Not so fast! You follow your amorous desire too far —you shouldn't let yourself be such a prey to passion. Aha! Mr. Man-of-Good-Will, you want to play one on me! How your soul gives way to temptation! Marrying my daughter and lusting for my wife! For a long time I couldn't believe my ears, and I kept thinking you'd change your style; but the proof has been pushed far enough. I'm satisfied and, for my part, want no more.

ELMIRE (*to* TARTUFFE): It was against my will that I did all this, but I was forced to the point of treating you that way.

TARTUFFE: What! You think . . .

ORGON: Come on, no trouble, please. Let's clear out of here with no more ado.

TARTUFFE: My plan . . .

ORGON: That talk is out of date; you must leave the house this very minute.

(TARTUFFE *starts to leave, crestfallen, then turns around and straightens up.*)

TARTUFFE: It's up to you to leave, you who speak like the master. The house belongs to me. I shall make it known, and I'll show you that people are wasting their time when they turn to cowardly tricks to pick a quarrel with me. I'll show you that there's an error in reckoning when you do harm to me, and that I have just what I need to upset and punish imposture, to avenge the offense to heaven and force repentance on those who talk of making me leave.

(*Exit* TARTUFFE.) (IV. 8)

ELMIRE: What kind of talk is that? What does he mean?

ORGON: My word, I am upset, and have no reason to laugh.

ELMIRE: What?

ORGON: I see my mistake from the things he said. That deed of gift disturbs me.

ELMIRE: The deed of gift . . .

ORGON: Yes, it's all done. But I have something else besides that worries me.

ELMIRE: What?

ORGON: You'll soon find out, but first let's see if a certain strongbox is still upstairs. (*Exeunt.*)

Act Five

(*Enter* ORGON *and* CLÉANTE.)

CLÉANTE: Where are you off to?

ORGON: Alas, how do I know?

CLÉANTE: It seems to me that we should first consider together what can be done in this case.

ORGON: That strongbox really upsets me; more than all the rest it puts me into despair.

CLÉANTE: That box, then, is some important mystery?

ORGON: It's a trust that Argas, that friend I feel sorry for, confided to me in great secrecy. When he fled he selected me for that; from what he told me, they are papers in which his life and his fortune are wrapped up.

CLÉANTE: Then why did you let them fall into someone else's hands?

ORGON: It was because of a case of conscience. I went straight to my traitor to confide in him, and his logic managed to persuade me that it would be better to let him keep the strongbox, so that in case of inquiry I could make a denial, and have at hand a subterfuge by which I could with a clear conscience swear an oath contrary to truth.

CLÉANTE: You are in a bad way; at least, so it appears to me: Both the deed of gift and the custody of this trust were, to tell you my own feeling, steps you took too rashly. With pledges like those he can lead you a merry chase. And since he had those holds over you it was even more imprudent to put pressure on him—you should have tried to find some gentler, more roundabout way.

ORGON: Oh! Under a fine appearance of touching fervor to hide a heart so deceitful, a soul so wicked! And I, who took him in, a penniless beggar . . . That does it, I renounce all

72

pious men. From now on I'll have a frightful horror of them —I'm going to treat them worse than a demon.

CLÉANTE: Well, now! Isn't that one of your fine fits of anger! You don't know what moderation means. Your reason never finds the right path, and you always rush from one excess to another. You have seen your mistake and realized that you were led astray by a sham zeal; but what reason requires you to mend your ways by falling into a greater error, confusing the hearts of all pious people with the heart of a treacherous blackguard? What? Because one rascal boldly tricks you with a high and mighty disguise of austerity, you think that everyone is made like him, and that there's not a truly pious person alive? Leave such stupid conclusions to freethinkers. Discriminate between virtue and its appearance. Never risk your esteem too quickly, and in that respect find the proper mean. Keep, if you can, from honoring imposture, but just the same do no harm to true zeal; if you have to fall into some extreme, it's better still to sin on the other side.

(Enter DAMIS.) *(V. 2)*

DAMIS: What, Father! Is it true that a wretch threatens you, that he blots all your kindess from his soul, and that his base pride, only too worthy of wrath, arms itself against you with your own gifts?

ORGON: Yes, my son, and it gives me untold pain.

DAMIS: Leave it to me, I'll cut off both his ears. Before his insolence we must not waver. It's up to me to set you free at one stroke, and, to settle this, I must strike him dead.

CLÉANTE: Isn't that just like a young man to talk that way? Please calm those noisy outbursts; we live under a reign and at a time in which violence is a poor way to conduct one's affairs.

(Enter MME PERNELLE, MARIANE, ELMIRE, DORINE.) *(V. 3)*

MME PERNELLE: What is this? I hear terrible mysteries here.

ORGON: These are innovations that my own eyes have witnessed, and you see the reward of my pains. I devoutly take in a man in his wretchedness; I house him and treat him like my own brother; every day I load him down with gifts; I give him my daughter and all my fortune; and at the same time the vile traitor makes a foul attempt to seduce my wife. And, still not satisfied with these base efforts, he dares to threaten me with my own gifts and sets out to ruin me by using advantages with which my own imprudent kindness has just armed him; he wants to drive me from the fortune that I have deeded to him, and reduce *me* to the level where *he* was when I rescued him.

Dorine: The poor fellow!

Mme Pernelle: My son, I simply cannot believe that he tried to commit so foul an act.

Orgon: What?

Mme Pernelle: Pious people are always the objects of envy.

Orgon: What do you mean with that talk, mother?

Mme Pernelle: In your house people behave in an outlandish way, and the hatred they bear him is only too well known.

Orgon: What does that hatred have to do with what you've been told?

Mme Pernelle:

    I told you a hundred times when you were little:
    Virtue in the world is hunted forever;
    The envious die, but envy, never.

Orgon: But what does this talk have to do with what happened today?

Mme Pernelle: They've probably made up a hundred foolish tales about him.

Orgon: I've already told you that I saw everything myself.

Mme Pernelle: Nothing is stronger than slanderers' malice.

Orgon: You'll make me damn myself, mother. I tell you I saw this brazen crime with my own eyes.

MME PERNELLE:

> Gossips always have poison to spread,
> And nothing is safe, living or dead.

ORGON: That's talking sheer nonsense. I *saw* it, I tell you, *saw*, with my own eyes, *saw*, what you call *saw*. Do I have to scream it in your ears a hundred times, at the top of my lungs?

MME PERNELLE:

> Appearance almost always deceives;
> One must not judge by what one sees.

ORGON: This is driving me wild.

MME PERNELLE:

> False doubt is a weakness of all kinds of people,
> And a good act is often construed to be evil.

ORGON: So I should construe as charity the desire to kiss my wife?

MME PERNELLE: Before you accuse people you need to have just causes, and you should have waited until you saw that you were sure of things.

ORGON: What the devil, Mother! What better assurance could I have? Should I have waited until, right before my eyes, he'd . . . You'll make me say something stupid.

MME PERNELLE: After all, his soul is smitten with a zeal too pure—I cannot bring myself to think that he tried to do the things they say.

ORGON: Really, I'm so mad, if you weren't my mother, I don't know *what* I might say to you.

DORINE: A fitting repayment, sir, of earthly things; you didn't want to believe and now you're not believed.

CLÉANTE: We are losing time in sheer trifles when we ought to be taking some steps. We must not nap in the face of the swindler's threats.

DAMIS: What! His impudence would go that far?

ELMIRE: For my part, I don't think that legal action is possible because his ingratitude would be too plain.

CLÉANTE: Don't count on it; he will have ways of making his efforts against you seem right. With less than that, a strong cabal can trap people in a maze of troubles. I tell you again: Considering how he is armed, you should never have put that much pressure on him.

ORGON: That's true, but what could I do? I couldn't master my resentment toward that traitor's pride.

CLÉANTE: I really wish we could arrange some semblance of peace again between you two.

ELMIRE: If I had known he had such weapons in his hands, I would never have given any basis for so much alarm, and my . . .

(V. 4)   (MONSIEUR LOYAL *appears at the door.*)

ORGON (*to* DORINE): What does that man want? Go find out right away. I'm in a fine shape to have people coming to see me!

M. LOYAL: Good day, dear sister. Allow me, I pray, to speak to Monsieur.

DORINE: He has company, and I doubt that he can see anyone now.

M. LOYAL:
    I have no intention of making an intrusion.
    My arrival, I think, will in no way offend him,
    And I come for something that he will find pleasing.

DORINE: Your name?

M. LOYAL: Just tell him that I have come on behalf of Monsieur Tartuffe, for his good fortune.

DORINE (*to* ORGON): It's a man with a mild manner who has come on behalf of Monsieur Tartuffe on some business which he says you will find pleasing.

CLÉANTE: You must see who this man is and what he wants.

ORGON: Perhaps he has come to reconcile us. How shall I act toward him?

CLÉANTE: Your resentment must not break out, and if he speaks of agreement, you must listen.

M. LOYAL:

    Greetings, monsieur.

    May your enemies burn in eternal fire,

    And may heaven favor you as I would desire.

ORGON: This mild beginning agrees with my judgment, and already foreshadows some kind of settlement.

M. LOYAL:

    Your whole house has always been dear to me,

    And your good father was often served by me.

ORGON: Monsieur, I am very ashamed, and beg your pardon for not recognizing you or knowing your name.

M. LOYAL:

    My name is Loyal, native of Normandy,

    Justice of the Peace, in spite of all envy.

    For forty years, thanks be to heaven,

    I have in all honor practiced that function,

    And I have come, with your kind permission,

    To serve you with a certain writ.

ORGON: What! You are here . . .

M. LOYAL:

    Monsieur, no anger:

    It's nothing but a little court order,

    A notice of eviction of you and yours,

    To move your goods and chattels, and make way for others,

    Without delay or hindrance, as it requires here.

ORGON: I! Leave this house?

M. LOYAL:

    Yes, sir, if you please.

    The house, you know, belongs at present

    To good Monsieur Tartuffe, without a question.

    Of your fortune he is henceforth lord and master,

    By virtue of a contract of which I am the bearer.

    It is in good form and cannot be contested.

DAMIS: This is surely great impudence—I am amazed.

M. LOYAL: Sir, I have no business to do with you. It's with Monsieur; he is both reasonable and gentle, and knows too well a gentleman's duty to wish to oppose the law in any way.

ORGON: But . . .

M. LOYAL:

> Yes, monsieur, I know that you will not
> Want at any price to try rebellion,
> And that you will allow me as an honest person
> To carry out here the orders I am given.

DAMIS: You might very well get yourself a piece of cane on your black apron, Mr. Justice of the Peace.

M. LOYAL: Make your son be silent or retire, monsieur; I should regret being forced to couch you in a bill of particulars.

DORINE (*aside*): This Monsieur Loyal has a most disloyal air.

M. LOYAL: For all gentlefolk I have great affection, and I only took these papers upon myself, sir, to do you service and pleasure, so that no one would be chosen who—not having the same zeal for you as I do—might have proceeded in a less gentle fashion.

ORGON: And what worse could a person do than order people to leave their own house?

M. LOYAL:

> You have some time; I will defer
> The execution of the order
> Until tomorrow, sir.
> I shall just come here and spend the night,
> With ten of my men, in peace and quiet.
> Before going to bed, for the sake of form
> You will please bring me the keys to your door.
> I shall take care not to trouble your rest
> Or permit anything not entirely correct.
> But tomorrow, early, you must be agile
> To empty this house of its least utensil.
> My men will help you—I chose them pretty stout
> To help you carry everything out.

I think no one could have treated you with any more
  kindness;
And, since I have acted with such great indulgence,
I entreat you also, monsieur, to behave with propriety,
That I may be nowise disturbed in my performance of
  duty.

ORGON (*aside to* CLÉANTE): Right now I would gladly give
a hundred of the finest gold crowns I have left to be able to
plant the hardest blow I could right square on that snout.

CLÉANTE (*aside to* ORGON): Hold on, let's not upset things.

DAMIS: His brazen nerve makes it hard to hold back—my
fist itches.

DORINE:
  With such a fine back—I say! Monsieur Loyal,
  A few blows with a stick would suit you quite well.

M. LOYAL:
  Those shameful words might be easily punished;
  Warrants are issued for women too, dearie.

CLÉANTE:
  Let's finish with this, monsieur; that's enough.
  Give us the paper quickly, please, and leave us.

M. LOYAL: Until we meet again, may heaven continue to
bless you! (*Exit.*)   (V. 5)

ORGON: May it confound you and the one who sent you!
     Now you see, mother, whether I'm right—you can judge
the rest by this writ. Do you admit his treachery at last?

MME PERNELLE: I am flabbergasted and dumbfounded.

DORINE: You complain and blame him without right or reason—this merely confirms his pious designs. His virtue reaches
its peak in love of his neighbor; he knows that wordly goods
often corrupt man, and, out of pure charity, he wants to spare
you any hindrance to salvation.

ORGON: Shut up; that's the word to say to you every time.

CLÉANTE: Come, let's see what plan you ought to choose.

ELMIRE: Go and make known his brazen ingratitude. That

form of action will make the contract null and void, and his unfairness will appear too foul to let him have the success you think.

(V. 6)   (*Enter* VALÈRE.)

VALÈRE: Regretfully, sir, I come to add to your burdens, but urgent danger forces me. A very dear friend of mine, who knows the grounds of my concern for you, violated for me, with thoughtfulness and tact, the secrecy which ought to be given affairs of state; he has just sent me information the consequences of which are that you are reduced to taking immediate flight. The scoundrel who has long deceived you denounced you to the king an hour ago, and among the attacks, put into his hands a strongbox belonging to an important political fugitive, which, he says, you have been guilty of keeping secret in spite of your duty as a subject. I don't know the particulars of what they call your crime, but an order is out for your person, and—the better to execute it—he himself is ·charged with accompanying the one who is to arrest you.

CLÉANTE: Now his claims are armed; that's how the traitor hopes to get possesssion of your fortune.

ORGON: I admit the fellow is a wicked beast.

VALÈRE: The slightest delay may be fatal. I have my carriage at the door to take you away and a thousand crowns which I have brought you. Let's not lose any time; this is a crushing blow—one of those that you can parry only by flight. Let me see you to a safe place and go with you the whole way.

ORGON: Alas, how much I owe you for your kind trouble! We'll have to await another time to thank you for it, and I ask heaven to favor me enough that one day I may reward this generous service. Farewell, take care, the rest of you . . .

CLÉANTE: Go quickly, dear brother; we will think about what has to be done.

.V. 7)   (*Enter* TARTUFFE *and the* OFFICER OF THE CROWN.)

TARTUFFE: Gently, sir, gently, don't run so fast; you won't

have far to go to find your lodging—you are arrested in the name of the king.

ORGON: Traitor, you kept this stroke for the last! Scoundrel, that's the blow you finish me off with—that's how you crown all your treachery.

TARTUFFE: Your insults have no power to provoke me; I am schooled to suffer all for the sake of heaven.

CLÉANTE: Great moderation, I agree.

DAMIS: With what insolence the cad makes sport of heaven.

TARTUFFE: All your tantrums cannot move me; I am thinking of nothing but doing my duty.

MARIANE: You have a great claim to glory from this, and your undertaking is very honest.

TARTUFFE: An undertaking cannot help being glorious when it stems from the power which has sent me here.

ORGON: But did you remember, ungrateful soul, that my hand rescued you from squalor?

TARTUFFE: Yes, I know what help I have received from you, but the king's best interest is my first duty; the righteous violence of that sacred duty stifles in my heart all gratitude, and to such powerful bonds I would sacrifice friends, wife, relations, and myself with them.

ELMIRE: The impostor!

DORINE: How well he knows the treacherous means of throwing about himself a fine cloak of everything we revere!

CLÉANTE: But if it's as perfect as you declare—this zeal which impels you and in which you deck yourself out—how does it happen that it decides to put off its appearance until he has caught you chasing his wife, and that you didn't think of going to denounce him until his honor forced him to drive you away? I don't mention the gift of all his fortune, which he had just made you, as something that should have changed your mind; but if you wanted to treat him as a criminal today, why did you consent to accept anything from him?

Tartuffe (*to the* Officer of the Crown): Deliver me, sir, from this shrilling, and kindly accomplish your order, please.

Officer of the Crown:
> Yes, I have stayed too long in the accomplishment,
> Your timely invitation asks me to fulfill it—
> To carry it out, follow me at once
> To the prison that is appointed for your keep.

Tartuffe: Who? I, sir?

Officer: Yes, you.

Tartuffe: Why to prison, then?

Officer:
> To you I have no account to render.
> (*To* Orgon) Sir, be at peace once more; the alarm is
>   past.
> We live under a prince hostile to fraud,
> A prince who sees clearly into every heart,
> Who is not deceived by the impostor's art.
> His great soul, with discernment provided,
> Gazes on all things with clearest sight;
> There no stealth finds furtive entrance,
> And his steady reason falls into no excess.
> To pious men he gives immortal glory;
> But without blindness his zeal shines forth,
> And his love for the true does not close his heart
> To a just horror of those who are false.
> Here was not a one to catch him unawares—
> He can defend himself from finer snares.
> Straight off, his brilliance pierced
> To the dark folds of that base heart.
> Come to accuse you, he betrayed himself,
> And, by an act of divine justice,
> Was revealed to the prince as a notorious swindler
> About whom he had information under another name;
> It is a long list of actions, every one foul,
> Which would form many a volume of accounts.

> This monarch, in a word, detested
> His base ingratitude and disloyalty to you;
> He has added these items to his other crimes,
> And allowed him to lead me here only
> To see his impudence go to the bitter end
> And make total satisfaction to you.
> Yes, all your papers, of which he says he is master,
> Are returned to you from the hands of this traitor.
> With sovereign power he breaks the bonds
> Of the deed which made him a gift of your fortune,
> And, finally, he forgives you that secret offense
> Into which a friend's exile caused you to fall;
> That is the prize he gives to the zeal which formerly
> You publicly proved in upholding his rights,
> To show that his heart knows how, when least we expect it,
> To pour forth the reward for a good action,
> That with him no merit is ever lost,
> And that, better than evil, he remembers the good.

DORINE: Heaven be praised!

MME PERNELLE: Now I can breathe again.

ELMIRE: What a fortunate outcome!

MARIANE: Who would have dared believe?

ORGON (*to* TARTUFFE): Ha ha, there you are, traitor . . .

CLÉANTE: Ah! Dear brother, stop—do not descend to indignities. Leave a wretch to his bad fate and don't add to the remorse that overwhelms him. Wish, rather, that this day his heart may make a blessed return to the arms of virtue, that he may mend his ways, detest his viciousness, and that he may soften the justice of our great prince; meanwhile, you will go down on your knees before his Graciousness and offer the thanks due for such gentle treatment.

ORGON:

> Well said. Now let us go before his feet with praise,
> Rejoicing in the kindness that his heart displays;

And with that primal debt discharged in part,
Then must we grant the claims of a noble heart,
And in sweet wedlock crown Valère,
Whose tender passion is true and fair.

(Curtain)

The Library of Liberal Arts